- Puppy Training Guide -

Raising The Perfect Pet

Dogology
Blueprint

The Stress Free Puppy Guide to Training Your Dog Without The Headaches

BULLDOGOLOGY PET SOLUTIONS®

WWW.BULLDOGOLOGY.NET

CONTENTS

Introduction

Bringing home a new puppy is a big first step. You are adding in a new addition to your home, and the whole dynamics are going to change.

Whether you already have kids and are introducing your new puppy to a big family or you are an individual who just wants a companion, training your puppy is really important.

This training helps the puppy to see what behaviors are approved in your home and which ones will get them in trouble.

It sets the boundaries for who is in charge and gives the puppy some meaning to feel confident and know they belong.

If you have never owned a puppy before, the idea of training them can seem daunting. You may have heard horror stories from your friends or family who had dogs who were always getting into the trash or causing some other issue.

As a pet owner, you want to have the dog who is well behaved and who will always listen to you. Perhaps these horror stories kept you away from purchasing the dog of your dreams for all this time. But now that you have brought the new puppy home, it is time to get to work.

Training your puppy does not have to be a big chore. But you do need to get started right away. Proper training starts from the moment you bring the puppy home.

You have to assert your dominance and not let the puppy get away with everything. In the eyes of your puppy, if you aren't showing them the rules and being in charge, they are the ones in charge. Once this happens, things can get even more challenging.

Starting with the training asserts that you are the leader, the alpha, the one in charge. The puppy will recognize this right away and follow all your commands.

Of course, lots of praise and some treats along the way can make this training session more fun for both you and the puppy.

This guidebook is here to help you out with all your training needs.

Whether you are brand new to owning a puppy or you are having some difficulties with a new addition to the family (and you've owned puppies in the past), this guidebook has all the tips that you will need to give your new puppy all the training that they need. From crate training to learning how to be the alpha to helping with obedience training, you will have all the basis covered to give your puppy the very best in training services.

Teaching the puppy commands is not all there is to the process though. We will also spend some time talking about how to properly care for your puppy while they live with you.

We talk about how to take them to the vet, what kinds of food are best to keep the puppy healthy and happy, and the importance of grooming. These are all important factors in helping your puppy to stay healthy so that they continue behaving and doing what you ask.

So when you're ready to begin training your new puppy and need some help getting started, take a look through this great guidebook. It is full of all the information that you need to give your puppy the best training and the best care possible so that you can have a happy and joyful home together.

Chapter 1
The Psychology of the Puppy

Puppies have a unique way of learning. They are going to learn in different ways, react with humans based on how the human acts with them, and will learn much better if you understand how these different pieces fit together.

Let's take some time to look at the psychology of the puppy and learn how this can make a huge difference in your training with the new puppy.

How Your Puppy Learns

The first thing you must remember when training a dog is that they are not humans. No matter how close you two get and what you try to do, the dog is not going to be human.

This means that you will not be able to train the dog in the same way that you or other humans have. In order to train your puppy, you must use the tricks that help a puppy learn.

Rather than through words and commands, the puppy is going

to learn more through scent and other visual cues. This is why most commands are given with a hand gesture rather than just the word.

Puppies are great at learning your body language to figure out if you are happy or if they are doing something wrong. There are some verbal communications, such as learning one or two word commands, but expecting the puppy to learn a whole string of sentences on their own will result in disaster.

So if you want to teach your puppy how to do certain tasks, you need to rely less on the verbal cues and more on your body language and your hand gestures.

You can incorporate a verbal command in with the hand gesture, something that is useful in emergencies or when the dog isn't looking at you, but keep the commands down to just a few words and use the hand gestures and other nonverbal communication to help train your dog.

Another thing that you must understand is that dogs need some direction. They need to know what is allowed in their little world, and when they don't have these clear cut rules, they are gong to get into trouble.

Have you noticed that your puppy is going to the bathroom all over the house, tearing up clothes and papers, and performing other naughty behavior even after you took the time to train them? This most often can be due to the fact that you aren't setting them up with some clear cut rules about their life.

Rather than seeing this as bad behavior, you need to see the reason behind this behavior and learn how to move it to a more approved method. For example, when the puppy is digging through your couch, shoes, clothes, etc. they are doing this because they need to hunt and to herd. If you are able to train them to do this in a new way, such as giving them their own toys to play with, taking them on a long walk, or give them some other approved tasks that will keep them out of trouble compared to just locking them up and not letting them get all this energy out.

Psychologists such as Skinner and Pavlov have spent a lot of time looking at the behaviors of dogs and how they respond to different situations. While these were used mostly to see how humans may respond when faced with different situations, but it provided a lot of insight into how puppies and dogs can be trained as well.

Through these studies, dogs are going to respond best to operant and classical conditioning.

First is the classical conditioning, which is basically the involuntary responses that the dog is not able to control; this would be when the dog salivates when they see dinner.

The other side is operant conditioning, which is the voluntary responses; this would include the dog learning how to sit or roll over because they want the promised treat.

If possible, you want to work on classical conditioning. This will use the involuntary responses of the puppy to help you to get the desired results. Some people will use this in order to get their puppy used to the idea of an object that they find harmful or negative. For example, you may want to put the dog in a harness to begin walking, but they are scared of the contraption. You can start to show the puppy right before they get started with dinner every night and soon they will see the harness associated with the meal. Over time, they will start to see the harness as a good thing.

Operant conditioning can be split up into two different techniques to shape how your dog is going to act.

There is aversive dog training where you will use positive punishment and negative reinforcement and then reward dog training that will use negative punishment and positive reinforcement. With this kind of conditioning, you are going to teach your dog to change up their behavior by either adding an aversive stimulus or taking it away.

In other situations, you can add a rewarding stimulus to help the puppy learn what you want them to do; the stimulus can be many things such as playtime, toys, food, and so on. An aversive stimulus can include a finger jab, a sound they don't like, or even an electric shock.

Each dog will respond to the stimulus in different ways. Some are easier to work with and may behave just by taking away the positive stimulus. For example, if you take away their play time, they will start to behave in order to get it back.

Other puppies may need more aversive punishments in order to behave in the proper way and learn where their personal boundaries are.

One thing to remember with this kind of training is that you should not give rewards to your dog too often. While it is fine to reward good behavior when it is exceptional, rewarding each time your puppy does something leads to them expecting it and they may refuse to do the action without the reward following.

Understanding how puppies learn is one of the first things that you must do in order to see success with your training. Seeing the puppy as human and trying to train them as such is not going to lead to very positive results. Take a step back and just see how the puppy is responding to your training techniques, and you will be able to learn which techniques are working the best for your methods.

Getting Along with Dogs and Humans

The relationship you form between you and the puppy is going to make a huge difference in how long the training is going to take and whether you are successful or not.

The first thing you have to get control of is who the alpha in your relationship is.

Dogs come with the pack mentality.

It does not matter if this puppy actually lived in a pack during their life or not, they are going to have this pack mentality and you will need to acknowledge this early on to help with the training. Because of this pack ideology, the dog needs to know that there is someone in charge.

Hopefully, you are able to establish yourself as the alpha dog early on. If you are successful, you will have a much better time training your puppy and you will experience fewer problems.

If you are not successful in being the alpha dog, your puppy will assume this position belongs to them. They will believe they are the ones in charge and will start to act out and try to control you. This is where issues with obedience, destroying the house, and other aggressive behaviors start to come out. Right from the moment you bring your puppy home, it is critical that you establish yourself as the alpha dog to make things easier.

How Long Does it Take to Train a Puppy

One question that many new dog owners have is how long it will take to train their puppy.

There are different aspects to this. Some dog owners want to know how many classes they will need to sign up with a professional before their dog is trained. Others are curious about how long they will need to train before they can leave the dog safely at home without a mess.

The answer is not that simple. While it'd be nice to have a set amount of days that the training will take and then it's all over, each dog is going to be different. There are also a number of factors that come into this process that will determine if the training takes a few weeks or a few months. Some of these factors include:

- The temperament of the dog—some dogs are really easy to train. You may spend a few days working with them, and then you are done for life. Other dogs may have difficulties in concentrating or understanding what you would like them to do. These dogs may take a bit more time to get the training down.
- How much time you devote to training—if you are able to take a week off work and devote a lot of time to training your puppy, you will see success faster than someone who can only devote an hour or so each day.
- How consistent you are with training—when it comes to training, you have to keep up with the training. You can't work on it during the weekends and then just let the puppy get away with anything they want during the week. Even if you just have a few minutes, keep up with the training each day.
- How consistent you are with rewards and punishments—rewards and punishments need to be consistent all the time. You can't say that something is bad one time and then just let the puppy get away with it later. This will confuse the puppy and add time to their training process.

If you are able to remain consistent with your training and work on it all the time, you will see results in a short amount of time and living with your new puppy will be more enjoyable for everyone.

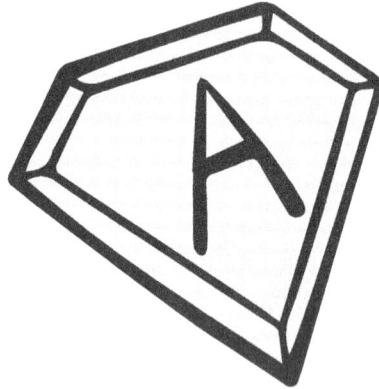

Chapter 2
The Importance of Being the Alpha in the Home

One of the first things you should do when you bring a new puppy home is become the *alpha dog*.

Puppies have a pack mentality right when they are born. They believe that one dog is the leader of the pack and that the rest of the group must follow along with this alpha to ensure the safety of all. The puppy is going to quickly start looking for the alpha in your home the moment you bring them into your life.

Ideally, you will establish yourself as the alpha dog right from the beginning. You will take the time to teach the puppy that you are the one who is in charge and that the puppy has to get your permission to do anything. If you are able to establish this order in your home, it is much easier to have a dog who behaves and training won't be such an issue.

For those who fail to become the alpha right out the door, you could be dealing with trouble. The puppy is going to search to figure out who is the alpha. If they aren't able to figure out anyone else in the family is the alpha, then they will assume that role falls to them.

Once a puppy assumes they are the alpha in the family, they are going to start acting more aggressive and working to get things their way. It can be really difficult to train a puppy to do your commands once they've decided to become alpha.

Let's take a look at some of the important aspects of being the alpha dog, why it is so important that you are the alpha in the relationship, and some of the tips that you can take to become the alpha with your puppy.

Determining The Alpha

Do you want a nice obedient dog who does what you ask and behaves all the time, or would you like a dog that breaks everything, tears up a lot of items, and is always trying to intimidate you? Determining who is the alpha early on is important to making a strong relationship between you and the puppy.

When the puppy comes into your home and isn't able to figure out who is the alpha, they give themselves this position. They become more aggressive and start to try and rule the house. They know, with their pack mentality, that someone needs to be in charge and keep things in line. And as the alpha, they are the ones who are in charge of keeping things in order. The puppy will start to act out, try to force you to do things you don't want to, and be pretty impossible to control without some hard work.

Dealing with a puppy who thinks they are an alpha can make training difficult. These are the puppies that start to destroy your house, may try to nip and bite at others, and will show other aggressive tactics.

It is always better to establish yourself as the alpha right when the puppy comes home rather than trying to convince the alpha puppy that they are no longer the ones in charge.

On the other hand, if you become the alpha, things can be much easier in the home. The puppy will look to you for guidance. They will try to stay in line in order to please you and to keep harmony in the home. They don't want to bring out your anger and they will want to work hard in order to please you.

Training will be a breeze because of the puppy's eagerness to make you happy. Your home will never be destroyed and training could get done in just a few days if you do this correctly.

So, it is always important that you are the alpha in the home. You should start this behavior and training from the moment you bring the puppy home. This may seem like a lot of extra work, but it can ensure that your puppy will behave and keeps you from having to deal with an aggressive alpha dog later on.

Tips to Becoming the Alpha

Knowing why being the alpha is so important is just the first step to establishing a good relationship between you and the new puppy. But you also need to follow some important steps to ensure that you are becoming the alpha dog in the pack.

Some of the best tips that you can try out to be the alpha dog and get the respect that you deserve from your new puppy include:

Taking a Walk

This is not the traditional walk that you see most humans taking their dogs on. This is the walk where the dog is pulling hard on a leash and the human is trying to control them from behind. This is going to teach the opposite of what you're looking for. Rather, you need to teach the dog that you are in control and they need to follow.

To do this, the dog should never be allowed to lead you during a walk. Instead, they need to either be beside you or behind you the whole time.

In the mind of your dog, the one who is leading is in charge, if the leader is you, that make you in charge. You should go on these walks at least once in each day until the dog is used to you being the one in charge. Not only will this help to establish you as the alpha dog, it will help to satisfy their migrating instinct and can get rid of all that pent of energy from being inside all day.

Eat Before the Dog

Many dog owners are used to just leaving the food out in the open and letting their dogs eat at any time. Others may choose to get the food set up for the dog before eating their own meal. This is not the way that things should be done if you want to be the alpha. In the pack, the alpha always eats first. If you want to be the alpha, you should be the one who eats first before the dog gets anything.

This is important even if you don't want to eat at that time. Every meal should show that you are the alpha and so even a quick little snack for yourself even if it's just a few bites, is often enough to get this to work out. This shows the dog that you are the most important, since the alpha always gets to eat first, and they are more likely to be subservient to you.

Avoid Table Scraps

If you want to be the one in charge, table scraps are not allowed to the dog. While it may be tempting to give them a nice little treat at the table or to do this to clear off some of your own work, this is going to show the puppy that they are equal to you. Only give the puppy their food during dinner time and have designated treats just for the puppy.

Have Scheduled Eating Times

It is easy to try and find ways that simplify your life, even when it comes to the care of your dog. One method that a lot of people use is a self-serving dog food container. This is nice because you just fill up the container every few days and your puppy can eat whenever they want. This saves you time and ensures that the puppy gets food when you are out of the house.

While this might seem like the perfect solution, it is actually going to make training your puppy so much more difficult. When he puppy gets to choose when they eat, they think they are the ones in charge. Remember that the alpha is the one who gets to make all the decisions. So if the puppy gets to make the decisions, they assume that they are the alpha. While this feeding container may seem like the perfect solution for your busy schedule, it is best to have eating times that are scheduled so the puppy eats when you say they can.

Entering the Home

Never let your puppy go through any doorway before you get to go.

You are the alpha, which means you are the most important and must show them who the leader is. When you come to a stairwell or to a doorway, make sure that the puppy goes in after you go through. If they try to go in before you, hold them back and give the command to stay. Once you are through the door, you can command them to com back through with you.

This may take a bit of time to teach the puppy the right commands, but it is all part of your training. Even when you first bring them home, don't let the puppy run through the door before you get a chance. Bring them back and hold them in the sitting position on the other side until you can walk through the doorway. Then you can let them go and allow them to come through the door. This may look a bit silly at times, but it is going to help teach your puppy that you are important and that they need to follow behind to stay out of trouble.

Don't Give Attention Right Away

Anytime that you leave the room or go out of the house, take a few minutes to ignore the dog when you come back. Giving them undivided attention right from the beginning lets them know they are important and deserver to get whatever they would like. Instead, when you ignore them, you let the puppy know that you will give them attention on your terms and when you feel the attention is warranted.

Simple Commands

Rather than just giving the puppy attention right when you come home, make sure they follow a simple command first. For example, you can ask them to sit or stay before you pet them or give them a hug after coming home from work. This puts the affection back into your hands rather than allowing the puppy to dictate when they get the attention. The command should be simple and not force the puppy to do some crazy tricks, but it's enough to establish that you are the one in charge.

Lying On The Floor

When it comes to lying on the floor, you should never do this with the puppy. The puppy belongs on the floor while humans belong on the couch and furniture. If you get down to the same level as the puppy, you run into problems with who is in charge. If you do allow the puppy on the couch, make sure that it is on your conditions. They should never be allowed to jump up on the couch unless you invite them and you are in charge of when it's time to get up.

In addition, if you come into a room and the puppy is lying in the way, never walk around them. This shows that you are worried about offending them and they start to assume they are the ones in charge. This can lead to aggressive behavior later on. Instead of walking around them, either force the puppy to get up and move for you, or just step over them.

Don't Let The Dog Sleep In Your Bed

While it might be tempting to allow your puppy to sleep in the same bed as you, this could end up in disaster when it comes to being the alpha dog and training them. When it comes to the pack mentality, the puppy sees the most comfortable sleep place as the one where the highest members of their pack gets to sleep. In your house, this would be the bed. If you allow the puppy to sleep on your bed without an invitation, they may start to assume they are one of the leaders of the pack as well.

In some cases, you may choose to allow the puppy to sleep on the same bed. If you do choose to do this, you must invite them up and they are never allowed to try and move any humans over or out of their way. You should make them be on the bottom of your bed to show that even though they are allowed to sleep here, they are still lower down in the pack.

Petting, Games, And Other Activities On Your Terms

Any games or activities that you do with your puppy should be on your terms. Never start petting a puppy because they were nudging into you or trying to get your attention. Never start a game of tug of war or fetch just because the puppy brought you a ball or started to harass you to play along with you. Once you start doing this, you have handed your power over to the puppy. If you want to put the puppy or play a game with them, you have to make it on your terms. For example, if they ask to be petted by nudging into you, command them to sit before petting them in order to turn it over to your terms.

Becoming the alpha dog in the relationship can be a big challenge for a lot of new pet owners. They want to establish a good relationship with their puppy early on, but feel that some of the techniques above are a bit strict and that they just won't be able to follow them. But if you want to have a good long relationship with your puppy, it is imperative to become the alpha dog as soon as possible and to maintain this position throughout the life of the puppy.

Chapter 3
Obedience, Manners, Behavior, Socializing, and Respect Training

Obedience is an important thing to teach your new puppy.

You don't want them jumping all over the place when company comes over, tearing up the house, or running out into oncoming traffic when you're out on a walk. It is best to start your obedience training right away so that the puppy knows what you expect out of them and you never have to worry about how they will behave in different situations. But how do you train a puppy, an animal that is full of energy and wanting attention, to obey you all the time? This chapter will take some time to explore the ways you can train your dog to be obedient so you know they will behave no matter what.

Steps to Help Train Your Puppy

Your puppy is basically a social animal. They like to be around other people and other animals as much as possible. This is why puppies do well coming into a new home and looking for a new way to behave. If you are good with your training and get started on it right away, you will find that it is easy to get the puppy to obey. They will know what is acceptable, where their boundaries lie, and they will work as hard as possible to please you.

But what happens when you fail to train them properly? What if you just bring the puppy home, play with them a bit, and then spend the next six months going to work and barely paying them any attention? When this situation happens, the dog is going to go back to their natural instincts of being an animal, rather than behaving in a manner that you would prefer. They will start to go through the house and soil it, they will get into your belongings and make a mess, bark at everything, and some puppies even resort to biting.

These are not good behaviors for a puppy. You are not going to be happy when your puppy starts acting like this, and when others get involved, things can get messy. But to a puppy who has not been trained on what is right and what is wrong, this is natural instincts. So with obedience training, it is your job to make sure that your puppy is not acting on these natural instincts. The puppy is never going to be able to completely get rid of these instincts, but with the proper training, you can help them learn how to direct this behavior into more acceptable behavior that you approve of.

In addition, the puppy loves having obedience training because it allows them to know where they belong in the social hierarchy. This gives them a direction and actually gives them more confidence. When the puppy knows how things work, they know how to act and what you won't allow at the same time. Once you are done with obedience training, you will find that the puppy can be given more freedom because they know the boundaries and they aren't going to try and cross these boundaries.

In order to accomplish this you need to quickly establish the hierarch in your home. You have to make sure that you are the one in charge and not the puppy. Your puppy is never going to listen to you as long as they have any idea that they may be the one in charge rather than you. Take control of the lead right from the beginning. Luckily, if you start the training at a young age, your puppy will be happy to take a subordinate role and they will see their obedience as a form of respect to you. Older dogs can still be taught how to follow your commands, but if they didn't get this training at a younger age, it is going to be a bit more difficult to accomplish.

During obedience, make sure that your puppy is having some fun and getting rewarded for their good behavior. Your puppy is not going to keep on behaving if you are punishing them or they get bored with the activity. Think back to when you were in school. Which teachers did you learn the most from; the ones who just sat there and barked their lecture at you or the ones who to your puppy.

While you are training, try to do this at your own home. Some people choose to hire a professional to help them to get down the basics. This is fine if you need a starting place, but in order to get the puppy to behave at home, you need to teach them the rules that have to be followed at home. If possible, have the professional come and work with you at your own home to make this transition easier.

Start the training in a room or area that your dog is familiar with. This allows the puppy to feel safe and secure while learning the new tasks and you will avoid the distractions of a brand new room. Once the puppy has learned and mastered some of the commands, you can move them to other areas so they learn that these commands apply no matter the location. But starting in a familiar room and keeping the training in this same area at the beginning can make everything easier.

Give the puppy some time to learn these commands and get comfortable with the new orders. Once that is done, you should try out some new scenarios so that the puppy can learn that they have to follow the rules no matter where they are. You can take them on a car ride, to the park, to a friend's house (make sure a dog is allowed first), and many other locations. This helps the puppy to gain more confidence because they are familiar with many different places. And they also learn that they have to behave and follow your commands no matter where they are. Soon, your puppy will understand that no matter where you take them, they have to behave at all times.

Training Rewards

This process cannot be all about telling the puppy what to do. You need to have some time in there that the puppy is being rewarded for the good behavior they are doing. If they are rewarded, with treats or praise, they are more likely to continue doing the commands because they want to continue getting your approval and attention. The reward is meant to help the puppy understand that by listening to you, they have done something right and it will provide them with the incentive to keep on going with that same behavior.

It is important to reward the puppy right after they do the correct behavior. If you wait too long, the puppy will not understand what you are trying to reward them for. Also, you need to be consistent with the rewards. Your puppy will not continue to do the correct behavior if you give them a reward one time and then forget to do it the next. The puppy will not understand that the reward is tied to the behavior, and you may as well get rid of the reward for all the good it is doing. You can get off the reward later on once the puppy has learned how to behave the way that you would like.

Punishment During Training

When it comes to training your puppy, you have to be really careful with punishment. While many think that punishment is the only way to get a naughty puppy to behave, it can often have the opposite effect and can make the puppy misbehave even more than originally. Over the long term, the puppy may become more aggressive and hard to handle if you use punishment too often.

This does not mean you should let the puppy get away with whatever they would like. You just need to be smart about the way you punish them when this happens. First off, any time that the puppy does what you would like, you should offer them a lot of praise. This helps the puppy to know that you really like what they are doing and they will continue on this path. Lots of praise now can save you a lot of hassle and trouble later. Plus, when you use a lot of praise, your reprimands will have more weight when you do need to use it.

If possible, redirection of a wrong behavior is a better course of action. If the puppy is getting into the trash, take them outside on a walk and praise them for listening to you. If they are jumping on the couch, redirect them to the floor and have them play with some of their toys. Make sure to praise them each time they do something that you like. This is more effective then reprimanding or punishing the puppy because it allows you to show the puppy what is allowed while also encouraging the good behavior.

When punishment is needed, start out with a sharper tone of voice. This should be sharp, short, and in control telling the puppy that they are doing something wrong. Never nag at the puppy when they are doing something wrong because they won't understand what this is all about. Usually, the sharper voice will be enough to get the puppy to stop their task and you can redirect them to something else.

In some cases, you can use the spray bottle technique to get the puppy to behave. This would be a mixture of lemon juice and water; the lemon juice irritates the dog a bit, but it is not going to harm them at all. When the puppy misbehaves, you can spray a bit of the water and lemon juice at their nose before redirecting them to a more appropriate behavior. The puppy won't like the spray, even though it isn't hurting them, and they will work to get the praise rather than your spray bottle.

One thing to keep in mind during this process is to never use physical violence around your puppy. Hitting, kicking, slapping, or spanking the puppy is never a good idea. This is not going to teach the puppy how to behave. Instead, it is going to teach your puppy that you are scary and eventually they are going to start acting out. Most aggressive dogs are the ones who come from families that used physical violence to get them to behave. If you have to punish your puppy, use the methods listed above and never resort to any type of physical violence to get them to behave.

Getting your puppy to follow your obedience training can be a challenge. They are going to have their own natural instincts and they will want to be the ones who are the leaders of the pack. But with some work and following the tips above, you can get your puppy to leave peacefully by your own rules.

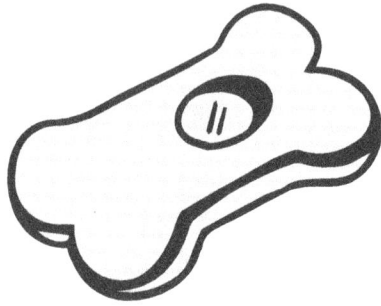

Chapter 4
Clicker Techniques

One popular method that is used to train puppies is the clicker. This tool makes it easy to get your puppy's attention and to have them behave in the way that you would like. Let's take some time to look at the clicker technique to see what this all entails and how you can use it to properly train your puppy

Getting Prepared to Use Clicker Training

Before you start using this on your puppy, you need to understand how to use the clicker. You will be able to purchase these from a pet store. It is a simple device that can fit into your hand and comes with some metal tongues that make a clicking noise when they come together. In order to get this to use as a training method, you need to learn how to push the clicker right when the puppy performs the correct behavior. In addition, the clicking sound should have some reward to follow whether that is verbal praise, toys, or food. Over time, the puppy will begin to associate the clicking sound with doing a great job.

The clicker should never be the reward for the puppy, but it should signal that you are going to give the puppy a treat when they behave. By using the clicker, you are teaching the puppy that they are doing the right thing by obeying you and that they are about to get a reward. When it comes to your puppy, this clicker is going to work better than verbal cues as you communicate during the training. This can make the training finish much faster than using your voice with them.

Once you purchase your clicker, you should introduce it to your dog. You need to teach the puppy what the clicker means. They are not going to act the way that you would like if you just bring it to training and expect them to act the right way. Bring the dog with you to a quiet room and hold out a treat in one of your hands and have the clicker in the other. Press your clicker one time, and then when the puppy looks at the click, hand over a treat.

For this to work, bring along quite a few treats; you will need to do this over and over until the puppy understands that the clicking noise means that they will get a treat out of the process. Don't give the puppy any treats in between the clicking noise or you will confuse them on this whole process.

While you are doing this, you should observe to see how the puppy is responding to the clicker. Some puppies may not like the sound of the clicker because they will see it as too harsh on their ears. You can try taking a towel and wrapping it around your clicker to see if this will help. Ballpoint pens can work the same way but have a lighter sound so you won't scare the puppy as much.

Training with the Clicker

Now that you have given the puppy some time to get used to the clicker and they understand that they will get a treat once they hear that clicking noise, it is time to get to the actual training with this device. To start, pick out a location that is quiet and won't have a lot of distractions for your puppy. Once you have given the puppy some time to get used to the clicking noise and how it works, it is possible to use it in louder locations, but start out small and at home. Use this as you are teaching different commands. Right after the puppy has done the command correctly, push the clicker and give them a treat or some praise as a reward.

One method that you can use with clicker training is known as "catching." With this process, you are going to click right when you see that the puppy is doing an approved behavior that they already knew how to do. For example, if you are in a room with the puppy and they lie down next to you, you can click as they are lying down and give them a treat. The puppy will probably get up to eat this treat, so wait until they lay down again and do the clicking process again.

The process of catching is only going to work when the puppy has already learned how to do a particular behavior without having to be commanded. But it is a good way to reinforce the good behavior so that the puppy doesn't start to fall off and not do the right things.

If you just brought the puppy home and haven't had a chance to train them at all yet, you should use the process known as "shaping." This is when you are going to use the clicker to help shape the behaviors that you want out of the puppy and you will do this at each stage of the process. For example, when working on lying down in a certain area, you will reward right as the puppy turns to go to that area, as they sit down, and then as they lay all the way down.

When you use the clicker at each of these spots, you are giving the puppy constant approval and rewards for doing a good job. This is the reinforcement that the puppy needs to see that their behavior is right and that they should keep on going with it. You may find that you will need to go over a new behavior several times before it is mastered, but the clicker method can make mastering the steps much easier.

Some dog owners choose to use the clicker as a type of food lure. Or this to work, you will use the treat in order to lure your puppy to do the right behavior. This method is used most often when you want to train your puppy how to lay down. For this to work, you will take the treat and hold it right above their nose before slowly moving that treat to the floor. While you may have o repeat this a few times, the dog is going to start following the treat to the floor. Once the elbows get to the floor, you will use the clicker and then give the puppy the treat.

Once the puppy has gotten the idea of putting their elbows to the ground, you can take away the food, but keep holding out your hand like you were before, like you are holding a treat. When the puppy does lie down, you can use the clicker before giving a treat. Eventually, you will be able to just use your hands to lure your puppy down to the floor without having to use the treat.

No matter which of these methods you use, adding in some verbal cues with the command can help you out. Eventually, you will be able to take out the clicker and the treats and simply use the words and a hand action to get your puppy to behave. This may take some time, but you should start using the verbal cue early on so that your puppy can start to associate the words with the action.

For this to work, you must keep the verbal cue direct and short. Just say a single word if possible and you should never use a sentence. The verbal cue needs to be given before the puppy does the command to teach them how to respond to your words. If you are using the lure method, you should give the verbal cue before you use your hand signal. When the puppy does what you ask with the verbal cue, make sure to use the clicker and give them a treat right away.

The clicker method is a really effective way to help your puppy learn how to follow your commands. It shows them that they have done a good job of listening and that they will be rewarded for that good behavior by praise or by a treat or toy. While you need to start out by giving them time to get used to the clicker and you may have to modify your methods to find the one that works with your puppy, this can be an effective way to quickly train your puppy to listen to your commands.

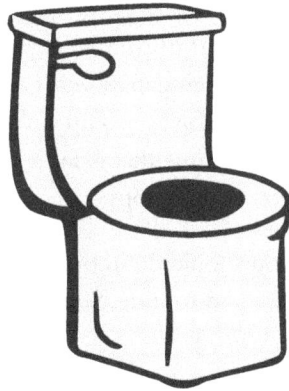

Chapter 5
Housebreaking Your Puppy

Housebreaking your puppy is often one of the most difficult things to do, especially if you are going to be gone all day for work or other engagements. But it is important to train your puppy where they are allowed to go to the bathroom in your home, whether you want them to go outside or in a small area on a puppy pad in your home. Often housebreaking is one of the first commands that you should work on with your puppy so that they can learn what is expected and fit in better. Let's spend some time looking at the best ways to housebreak and potty train your puppy in no time.

Set Up Your Routine

In order to help your puppy get potty trained, you need to set up a routine with them. This helps the puppy to understand what they are supposed to do during the day and when they are going to for sure be allowed to go outside. Just like humans, puppies also like to have some sort of routine in place in order to feel secure and to have some anticipation for what will happen next. Even though you aren't able to set up a routine that will stay the same all the time, having one that is fairly regular can make potty training much easier on the puppy.

So the first thing you should do in order to help housebreak your puppy is to set up a good routine. Some ways that you can do this include:

- Keep in mind that your new puppy will need to go potty often. Puppies have small bladders and won't be able to hold it for long. This means that you will need to take them out often when you first bring them home. Don't get frustrated when you have to go out with the puppy all the time and understand that they will learn how to control it better, and have to go less often, as they get older.

- Regulate when they eat—this is going to make it easier to figure out when they need to go out. If you leave the water and food out all the time, they are going to eat whenever they feel like it and you may not be ready when they need to go out. Have certain times that are meant for eating, and then watch to see how long after they eat that they need to go to the bathroom.

- Learn how often—each puppy is going to be different in regards to how often they need to go out. When you learn how often the puppy needs to go, it becomes easier to help them learn how to go out.

- Learn about the den instinct—the den instinct is when your puppy is going to feel some reluctance to soil the area that is their den. At first, they won't see the home as a den, but if you help them to learn that this is their home and their safe place, they are going to be more reluctant to soil up the home.

- Choose the bathroom—ideally, you will have the backyard be this place. But if you are in an apartment or another location that does not have a backyard or makes it hard for the puppy to get outside quickly, you may need to use some puppy pads and have a designated area for the puppy to do their business on.

Once you set up a routine, it becomes easier to help your puppy learn how to be potty trained and not go all over the house. This may take some time, but it is going to save you a lot of hassle later on.

Teaching the Puppy Wrong from Right

To help your puppy learn how to be potty trained, you will need to help them know what behaviors are approved and not approved in your home. One of the things that you need to train them is that going inside the house is not something that is allowed, but when they go in one of your designated areas or outside, they are doing something that you approve of. In order to help your puppy learn what is right and wrong, with potty training and with any other training process you are going with, try some of these tactics:

1. Maintain your routine—without the routine, your puppy is going to be lost and not understand what you expect of them. Follow the same routine with potty training each time; this means use the same spot to go, take them out the same door, give the praise each time, and so on so they begin to know what to expect. Soon they will start to understand what they should do and they will remember it.
2. Use encouragement—when it comes to potty training, encouragement is everything. When the puppy holds out and waits to go outside rather than inside, praise them. When they go in the right spot when you take them outside, praise them. Soon the puppy is going to look

for even more praise, they like to be noticed, and they will go outside each time.

3. Help them out—with a small puppy, they sometimes aren't able to make it to the right spot. Or they may be tired after a nap or in the morning and might not be able to discover the right spot to go in. You can help them out by picking the puppy up and putting them into the right area. Soon they will be able to do this on their own.

4. Use your voice to tell the puppy when they're wrong. Use a stern voice that reprimands the puppy so they understand that they did something wrong. They will try to avoid this voice the next time and be more likely to go in the right spot.

5. Choose a negative reinforcement—this can work along with your voice to encourage the puppy to stay away from the unacceptable behavior. Don't resort to hitting the puppy since this can just make them aggressive in the long run. A better choice is to use a spray bottle filled with some water and a bit of lemon juice. This lemon juice can irritate the puppy, but won't hurt them. The next time that you see the puppy going to the bathroom in an unapproved area, you can spray a bit of this on them to discourage their activity.

6. Take walks—sometimes puppies will go inside the house because they have a lot of pent up energy. Consider going on at least one decent sized walk each day. This can help the puppy let out some of this energy, and it is often good at loosening up the puppy so they have a better chance of going outside.

Once the puppy learns what is acceptable in your home and what activities you won't allow, it is easier to train them to behave. This is going to take some time and some patience, but soon you will have a well behaved puppy who is ready to do what you ask and who will go to the bathroom outside.

Potty Training When You Are Gone

Unless you are able to take off a few weeks from work in order to potty train your puppy, there will be times you have to leave the house during this training period. This does not mean that you should just hope the puppy will catch on to the training at night time and the weekends. You just need to think smart and provide ways to help the puppy train, even if you are not at home all the time.

One thing that you can try out is a playpen. For this, you will need to find some gates or other barriers that create a safe barrier for your puppy to play in. You will place this in a nice corner of the home and the puppy can play there all day while you are gone. During this time, they are not going to have control over their bladders at all and you will probably have a mess all over the pen when you come home. But, it is enough to keep the mess in one area and teaches the puppy that they are allowed to go in this area, but not all over the house. You just need to clean up the area when you get home so it is ready to go for the next day.

Over time, using this will become more comfortable to the puppy. They will learn that they should go in just one little area to do their business, rather than doing it all through the playpen. While it is not as good as them going outside, it allows the mess to stay in just one part of the playpen instead of all over the house.

Puppy Pads

Puppy pads are a great way to help potty train your puppy as well. You can use this along with the playpen idea that is above, but the puppy pads can allow you to eventually let go of the playpen and let your puppy roam the house while you are gone without having accidents all over the place. **Bulldogology Puppy Pads** are great for all dogs and can help to train your puppy to just go in one area while you're gone.

1. Select a suitable area inside your home where your pup will be eliminating. Make sure to place the puppy pad with the quilted side up.
2. When your pet starts to show signs that it needs to go, take your pet to the puppy pad and encourage your pet by using commands words (i.e. "Go pee! Good boy!") If your puppy eliminate in a different area of your home, lead your pup back to the pad. Repetition is key.
3. Once the pad is full absorbed, pick the pad up from each of the four corners to conceal it, and then carefully throw the pad away. Make sure to wash your hands after.
4. When your puppy becomes comfortable using the training pads regularly, start moving the pad outdoors to get him used to going outside.
5. Do not punish your pet for accidents - this can be very frightening for them and give you huge setbacks in training the pup. A gentle voice with positive encouragement will go a long way.

These puppy pads are nice because over time, you can get rid of the crate idea. Since the puppy has learned how to do their business on the puppy pad, they will keep this in mind, whether they are in the house or not. You can take them out of the crate and let the puppy have a bit more freedom while you are gone. You simply leave the pad in a corner that's acceptable for the puppy, and they will only relieve themselves here rather than all over the house.

Chapter 6
Crate Training

One method of training that many dog owners choose to use is crate training. This is great because it allows you to use the natural instincts of the puppy to your own advantage. The puppy is going to naturally want to make a little den for themselves. This is a place where they feel comfortable and can go to anytime they become scared or uncomfortable with a situation. With crate training, you can make the crate into the safe den place to help your puppy.

Keep in mind that when using crate training, you should never use the crate as a place for punishment. This is not somewhere to put the puppy when they are being naughty. Rather, it is a safe little place for them to go in order to learn new tricks and when they are feeling scared of the situation. If you turn this into a place of punishment, you will end up with a puppy who won't do anything in the crate.

To start, you need to pick out a good crate. Pick one that is going to be big enough to fit your puppy; big puppies get a bitter crate. Consider the future as well. If the puppy is going to get really big, pick out a bigger crate so that they are able to still use this safety place when they are older. Once you have the crate, take some time to pick out a place where you can permanently place the crate. You don't want to move the crate around too much or you can confuse the puppy. Picking out some blankets and a few toys can help the puppy feel safer and will give them a bit of entertainment when you aren't able to be home while they are in the crate.

Introducing the Crate

Once you have the crate all set up, it is time to introduce your puppy to the area. You need to do this slowly as the crate should be a safe and comfortable place for your puppy rather than one they are scared of because you tried to force them inside. Letting the puppy look at the crate and explore it a bit can help them to feel more comfortable with it and will eventually help them to be ready to stay there for longer periods of time. Some steps that you can take to ensure that you are introducing the crate properly to your puppy include:

- Don't use force—while you may be in a hurry to have your puppy like the crate, forcing them into it and then locking them inside can be a poor choice. Let them explore around and get used to the idea before leaving them inside. Also, never use the crate as a way to punish the puppy. This is a safe and positive environment; find other forms for punishment.

- Let the puppy "discover" the crate—one way that the puppy can become more comfortable with their crate is if they find it on their own. To do this, place the crate in the room you plan to leave it and then restrict the puppy to this area. Allow the puppy to sniff around and explore until they come upon the crate on their own. This can make it more appealing and they can feel proud for their discovery. Consider putting some treats, comfy blankets, and fun toys inside to help entice the puppy.

- Leave the door open—during the introduction phase, don't close the door. You can allow the puppy to come in and out of the crate and explore as they wish. Later on you may wish to close the door, but wait until your puppy feels comfortable first.
- Lots of praise—when your puppy finds the crate and begins to explore it, takes the time to praise them a lot. If you see that the puppy is heading over to the crate, take the time to praise them some more. When you use praise, you are teaching the puppy that they are taking the right steps to making you happy.
- Use some treats—sometimes it is difficult to get the puppy to go inside the crate. Use any enticements you can to help them out, including treats. This is often enough to get the puppy over to the right area and exploring the crate.
- Mealtime—if you need some more help with the crate, consider bringing mealtime to the crate. You can place the food inside the crate and allow the puppy to eat there. Make sure that the door stays open the whole time.
- Closing the door—this is going to be a slow process, but over time the puppy will feel safe in their crate and it is possible to close the door. Do this in increments. Try out closing the door while your puppy is eating and leave it closed for a few minutes after they are done. Over time you will be able to leave the door closed for longer times without an issue.
- Create your command—while training, come up with a command that tells your puppy to go into the crate. This should not be done when you are angry or upset with the puppy, but the command can be useful when you're heading out the door and need the puppy to be safe while you're gone.

The introduction period is one of the most important for this training method to begin working. This helps the puppy to become comfortable in the area and they are more likely to go back there whenever they need some comforting or you are going to be gone.

Acclimation

The goal of this crate training is to help your puppy have their own little safe haven when they are scared or you are out of the house. This means that once you are done with the introduction phase, you need the puppy to be comfortable with going inside the crate and not feeling abandoned or like they are forced into the crate. Some tips to help your puppy to acclimate to this crate includes:

- Stay home—at the beginning, you should be home during crate training. This helps the puppy to see the crate as more of a safe haven rather than some place they are going to be abandoned in. Whether you have to take a few days off work to accomplish this or you just choose to start training after work, make sure you are home at the beginning.
- Show encouragement—the puppy needs to know that the crate is safe and good for them to get in to. You can show encouragement with a lot of praise or offering them a treat any time they go into the crate.
- Stay consistent—if you choose to just use the crate occasionally, it is impossible for the puppy to get used to the idea. You need to use it on a consistent basis or you are wasting your time.
- Start leaving the room--Once your puppy begins to get used to their crate, it is time to get out of the room. Start with a few minutes first. Leave the room, and then come back in. When you come into the room, make the puppy wait a minute or two before you let them out.
- Increase your away time—this is going to take some time, but slowly you can spend more time away from the

crate and the puppy. Do this several time through the training session, adding more minutes each time you go away. This helps the puppy to learn that you are not present, but they will be just fine. When you come back into the room, don't let the puppy out while they are whining, or they will learn this behavior the next time around.

The acclimation period does take a bit of time. The puppy wants to be able to get out and play with you rather than being stuck in a crate all day long. But with some work and being consistent with your training, the puppy will soon see this as a safe zone and won't mind as much when you leave the room.

Leaving

Your goal with all of this is to teach the puppy how to be fine in the crate when you go out of the house. This is true whether you plan to leave the house just to run some errands or to go to work each day. Getting from just a few minutes to hours at a time can be difficult, so take it slowly and work at the pace that is best for your puppy. Some puppies are able to learn this pretty quickly and don't mind being left behind while others are going to get nervous when they are alone.

After you are able to get out of the room and stay gone for 30 minutes or more, and the puppy is handling it well, it is time to go out of the house. Start with a short leave to get some errands done or to do a quick jog around the block. For the first bit, only be gone for up to an hour. After a month, you can be out of the house for at least 4 hours.

During this time, you should vary how long you are gone and how long the puppy has to remain inside their crate. For the first time you could be gone for 5 minutes and then the next time go with 15 and so on. This helps the puppy to get used to you being gone for different times and they won't start to get nervous if you're gone for a longer period the next time.

Never make a big fuss when you leave the house or when you come back in. As you are preparing to leave for an errand or work, you should ignore the puppy for at least the last few minutes. Leave quietly and without saying anything to the puppy. Once you come back home, don't give your attention to the puppy right away. Take off your shoes and coat, put the groceries away, and do those tiny things you need to get done before turning your attention back to the puppy. When you are done, you can check on the puppy. If they are whining and making a fuss, keep them in the crate until they calm down. Once they are able to calm down, you can let the puppy out.

As soon as you let the puppy out of their crate, make sure they go outside. They have probably been inside the crate for some time and need the chance to go relieve themselves, or they will do it inside your home. This is also a good time to praise them for doing so well with potty training and waiting to go outside.

The process of leaving is going to take some time. But with the right hard work and dedication, you will be able to leave your puppy in a safe and secure place where they are comfortable while you get your errands done or go to work.

Night Training

It is not uncommon for dog owners to choose to use the crate even at night. The crate has already become a comfortable place for the puppy to be safe and they probably are already used to sleeping in it at some point in the day. It allows the puppy to get used to the crate as well, making night training the perfect way to kick off your crate training endeavors. If you would like to get started with night training, keep these things in mind:

- Quiet—while there might be a lot of traffic and noise in your home during the day, make sure that the crate is kept somewhere that is safe and quiet at night. This will help the puppy fall asleep rather than wondering what all the noise is. Consider setting up the crate so it's easy to clean out in the morning if placing a brand new puppy inside.

- Comfortable—your puppy will want a comfortable place to sleep, even if you're using crate training. Keep some blankets or a nice pillow inside so they can get a good night sleep.

- Do some exercise—it is not a good idea to keep the puppy inside the crate for a long period of tie in the day and then again at night without giving them some exercise. Your dog needs to move around and get a good workout. This is where walking and playing can help you out.

- Don't give in to the crying—the puppy is going to try and get your attention in the beginning, even at night. They would rather cuddle up next to you on your bed rather than stay in the crate. Don't give in. Make sure they have all the necessities they need and then ignore the whining. Eventually they will tire out, especially if you helped them exercise, and they will give up and go to bed.

- Give them bathroom breaks—this is especially important with brand new puppies who are being potty trained. They are not going to be able to hold their bladders all night long and you will have a lot of accidents if you don't take them out a few times. No puppy wants to sleep in their own filth. Take them out a few times each night and clean up the crate if an accident does occur.

- Consider leaving door open as they age—once the puppy has gotten trained on how to use the crate, you can consider letting the door stay open. This helps the puppy to get out on their own if they need to move a bit or to go outside. It can also make the crate more inviting if the puppy doesn't feel trapped in there all the time.

Crate training is a great way to work on training your puppy and getting them to act the way that you want. It provides the puppy with a safe and comfortable location to hang out during the day or at night while you are away and keeps them from feeling abandoned or alone. While it will take some time and effort on your part to make this all happen, you will be happy with the results when you're done.

Chapter 7
Puppy Tricks and
Command Training

One of the most enjoyable things that you can do with your
puppy is to train them how to do some tricks. While leash
training and potty training are useful to having a happy home
with a new puppy, teaching them how to do tricks can be a fun
thing to do during their play time and can be a blast for children
to help out with. While these tricks aren't necessary to have a
well trained puppy, they can make life with a new puppy a lot of
fun. This chapter is going to take some time to look at how to do
the basic commands with your puppy to get some amazing
results and some quality bonding time with the new puppy.

5 Commands to Try With Your Puppy

Sit

One of the first commands that dog owners try with their
puppies is to sit. Sitting should be considered a form of
politeness with your puppy and it is pretty simple for them to do.
You will find that this is a good command to use when guests

come over, rather than letting your puppy bounce all over the place and get in your guests' faces. The puppy can learn how to do this to show passivity to people coming into your home, and with some practice, they will learn how to do this to show patience when you are busy and can't help them at that moment.

When you want to start out with this command, you should start by standing right in front of your puppy. While saying this command, take out a treat and hold it right over their nose. The puppy is automatically going to put their butt on the ground when their head goes up to get the treat. Even though this is more involuntary compared to actually understanding what is going on at this time, you should still take the time to praise your puppy once they sit down and give them the treat. With some practice, the puppy will start to see that there is a connection between the action and the words and will be able to do this command even without a treat in hand.

You should not give out a treat each time that the puppy sits, or you will never get them to do the command without a reward. At first, you can use the treat to teach the command, but over time, you will need to use the treat less and less often and instead use a hand signal. For example, once the puppy has mastered the sit command, start handing out a treat only half the time and using the hand signal the other half. Over time you will be able to get the puppy to sit without having to give them a treat. Do this tip with all of the commands that you teach the puppy.

Stay

Teaching the puppy to stay is going to be useful at times. You may not want them to follow you out of the room or to leave the house when you do. You may be worried that they will try to run off when you are at a busy intersection. Teaching the puppy how to stay in one spot can really make things easier on you.

To begin this command, you should get your puppy to go into a sitting position while you are standing in front of them, with the puppy to your left side. Have the puppy face in the same direction as you for this command. Now, grab onto their collar gently and then give them the stay command. While giving this command, you can place an open hand right in front of your puppy's face with the tips of your fingers going up and the pam facing towards your puppy, kind of like making a little cup at the nose of your puppy. Hold this for a few seconds. If your puppy is successful at staying put, give them a reward and a lot of praise. If the puppy doesn't understand the command and tries to get up and move, you should get them to sit down again and give it another try. It is going to take a few times, but soon the puppy will associate the hand movement with the command and behave how you wish.

At first, you will only be able to get your puppy to sit still for a few seconds at a time. This is fine as you are just working on getting the puppy used to the command. Slowly start to increase the amount of time that your puppy should stay in one place after they have learned the command. In no time, your puppy will learn how to stay put until you ask them to come to you.

Down

Puppies like to bounce and get to know people. They like to show people affection and all their energy. But no one wants to come into your house and be attacked by a dog, no matter how friendly the dog's attention or how small the dog. This is why it's so important to teach the puppy the down command. With the right training, you probably won't even have to use this command at all as the puppy will sit and be patient with the guests, but in case they forget, or when they are young and full of energy, the down command can really help you out.

The down command is used the most often in order to tell the puppy their actions are not appropriate. It is meant to stop them from doing something, such as bouncing on a guest, if they happen to forget what the rules of the house are all about. When the puppy knows this command, it will only take one word to get them to behave.

To begin the down command, you should get the puppy into the sitting position. As you say the down command, you can place the left hand across the head of the puppy, making sure that your palm is down to the floor. You should also have a treat in the other hand and lower this to the floor at the same time, keeping it close to the puppy. The puppy is at first going to go after the treat; as soon as they get both of their elbows and their butt down to the floor, give them the treat and praise them. You will have to go over this step a few times to help them understand the connection between the command and the action, but they will learn quickly.

Come

At times, you will need the puppy to go in a certain direction. You may want to tell them which way to go on a walk. You may need them to come from another room to follow you or to get into their crate. This command is also a good way to tell them they are allowed to get out of one of the other positions, such as sit and stay, that you practiced earlier. This command will need to have an encouraging voice as well as a gesture to help the puppy feel secure in coming with you.

To get started on this one, have the puppy get into a sit or stay position across the room from you. Place a treat or some food for the dog at your feet and point with it. Say the command "come" encouragingly to the puppy a few times. The puppy is soon going to be drawn to the food and will start to head your way. After practicing this sequence a few times, and getting a ton of praise and attention from you, the puppy is going to learn how to come just by hearing the command and seeing your hand gestures.

Shake

Shake is a great command to teach your puppy while you are working on all the other ones. It can be fun to see your dog shake with puppy and your guests may appreciate the extra politeness. For this command, you should have the puppy be in their sit position. Stand right in front of your puppy and have your hand in a fist, making sure there is a small treat inside your fist, but not letting the puppy get to it. When the puppy is paying attention to you, offer out your hand. In the beginning, the puppy will just sniff at your hand and try to get at the treat, but once this is not successful, they will try to paw at the treat.

When the puppy starts to pay at your hand, you can give the puppy a treat, but give it from the opposite hand that the puppy is pawing at. Over the time, the puppy is going to start pawing at your hand, regardless of if there is a treat in there, each time you offer up the hand to them. Once this is a consistent practice, you can start to change out of the fist and offer up your hand until the puppy is willing to paw at the open hand like they are shaking. When they do this correctly, you can offer them up a shake.

After some time, you can start to add in a verbal cue to go with the shake. This may take some time for the puppy to understand, but soon they are going to associate the handshake with the verbal cue. You will be able to get them to give you a handshake without offering any treats once they start to associate the verbal cue with the actions. Make sure that at all stages of this process, you are offering up a lot of praise to the puppy for doing the right movements.

Tips for Successful Command Training

Training your puppy to do these basic commands is important to show your dominance and to add some structure to our training sessions with the puppy. But it is important to go about this process in the proper way. Some tips that you can follow to ensure that your puppy is going to do well with the training include:

- Do lots of rewards—your puppy likes to be rewarded for a good job. The more praise, as well as treats, that you give the puppy during the training process, the more success you will see. When the puppy is rewarded in this way, they are going to understand that they are doing something good, something that you want them to do. This encourages them to do the activity again until they have it mastered.

- Have training in the same place—in the beginning, you should have your training sessions in the same place, whether it's in the same room, outside, or wherever works for you. This helps the puppy to feel safe and get used to the command. Once the puppy is better at the commands, you can start to move the commands to other locations.

- Keep out distractions—your puppy, just like a small child, is going to be easily distracted. When they are distracted, it becomes much more difficult for them to get the commands down right. Try to get rid of all the extra energy in the puppy before beginning and do the command training in a location they will be free from a lot of distractions.

- Start the puppy early—the earlier you start out with this training, the easier it is to get the training done. This is because you won't have to break old habits in the process. Of course, if you have an older dog, or you missed out on those early months with a puppy, it is still possible to train your dog. The process is just going to take a bit longer to complete.

- Be patient—you are not going to be able to teach your puppy how to do all these commands in one sitting. They are not going to catch on that quickly and you will just become frustrated trying to make it happen. Be patient and let your puppy learn at their own pace.

Training your puppy to understand commands is an important step to building a good bond with your new puppy. Follow some of the steps in this guidebook to ensure that you are helping your puppy learn how to behave while having some fun with them during the process.

Chapter 8
How to Train a Puppy Not to Bite

It is a natural habit for your puppy to want to nip and bite at things. They don't understand that this is a bad thing and isn't acceptable when you first bring them home. They think it is a way to play or show their dominance, and some may perform this activity when they become scared in your new home.

It is important for you to stop this biting as soon as possible or the situation is just going to get a whole lot worse. The longer you wait to break your puppy of the biting habit, the bigger challenge it will become. Luckily, it is fairly easy to break this habit, especially in young puppies, simply by showing them that the biting is not approved and reinforcing other positive habits and behaviors like you are already doing in your obedience training. Start out early with the no biting rule, and then move on to some of the more fun activities, like teaching them how to do tricks.

Understanding Why a Puppy Bites

Before you can get your puppy to stop biting, you need to have the basic idea of why they have started the habit in the first place. When you first bring a puppy home, it is normal for them to want to bite while they grow. They have to learn that biting is not appropriate, either from you if they are an only puppy in the home or from an older dog in the pack, if you have more dogs around.

If you do have other dogs in the home, it is easier to get this training done. Your puppy is going to try and play with the other dog, having fun, wrestling, and starting to learn what behaviors are appropriate in your home. This is the time they will learn that biting is not acceptable. When the puppy is unsuccessful at controlling their biting during play, the older dog is not going to take it. They will often punish the puppy, remember that the dog may not be the alpha, but they are still higher up in the pack than the puppy, and they can give a more serious bite that could cause a bit of injury to get the puppy to stop. Most puppies are going to catch on easily to the idea that biting is bad, and you will have them trained up in no time with the help of your other dogs.

When this is your first puppy or you don't have any other dogs in the home, it is up to you to train the puppy not to bite. Some dog owners assume that it is not all that important to teach their dog that biting is bad. They assume that other dogs around their puppy will teach this skill or that the puppy will just grow out of the phase. Refusal to teach your puppy how to behave in terms of biting is going to result in a dog that is out of control with biting.

When the puppy is never taught that biting is bad, they are also not taught how to control the biting. These dogs often have a lot of behavioral issues when they get a bit older. If you feel that the puppy is not biting because you trained them improperly, but rather they are biting because they are angry or scared, you may need to bring in a specialist. This person can help you to figure out why your dog is biting, even if the dog knows that biting is bad.

Keep in mind that it is never acceptable for your puppy to bite at other animals or people. The only time this should be allowed is if they are really in physical danger and there is no other way for the puppy to defend themselves. This is not usually something that will happen, so you must teach your puppy that biting is bad and they are never allowed to use this technique.

Using some precautions during the training program can really help you out when it comes to teaching your puppy how not to bite and keeping others safe. A muzzle will work great if you have a puppy who is fond of nipping and biting at other people. Learn how to use the muzzle properly though or you could end up making the dog more aggressive rather than seeing results with this. Over time, the dog will learn that when they bite and misbehave, the muzzle will come out but if they are able to listen to your rules and do what you ask, you will take the muzzle off them.

Teaching the New Puppy That Biting is Bad

It is your job as the alpha in the pack to teach the new puppy that biting is really bad. The first thing that you should do in this case is to find a consistent way to react when your puppy bites. If you don't react the same way each time, the puppy is going to become confused as to whether they are doing the right steps to please you or not. When the puppy bites you, use a firm voice and say No! before walking away and ignoring your puppy. Time outs and social isolation are often good ways to teach the puppy that they have done something wrong since they are social animals and like lots of attention.

Another option is to let out a little yelp when the puppy is biting you. When the puppy is in a pack, their siblings are going to cry out a bit if one of the other puppies bites them too hard. When you yelp, you are giving out the same kind of signal that they would get if they were still in the pack setting. You can teach your children how to react to the puppy. Show them that shrieking, flapping their hands, or running is not acceptable. These activities are going to engage your puppy's instincts and can make the issue worse. Teach your child that they need to be clam and not react in a negative way when the puppy bites them.

Taste Deterrents

One thing that some people will use to make sure the puppy does not bite them is a taste deterrent. Before you get down and start playing, you can spray a bit of this deterrent onto your body as well as clothes, especially if these are items the puppy likes to rough house with. When the puppy is biting at you, don't move so they can get the full effect of this taste deterrent. Once they find out that the taste is pretty awful and they stop biting you, praise them for being good and then go on with playing.

There are a few different options that you can choose when it comes to the taste deterrents. Some options include white vinegar, tea tree oil, Vick's Vapor Rub, and bitter apple. These are not going to harm your puppy, but they will leave an unpleasant taste in their mouths so they won't like to bite as much. Make sure that you take the time to wash your hands off when you are done with the training session.

Teething Toys

Sometimes the puppy may be biting because they are going through the teething process. This is often painful and they need a bit of help with it. Make sure that your puppy has calmed down a bit before stroking them down and talking to the puppy. Keep the hands away from their mouth during this time and start playing them using some teething toys. You can play fetch to get out some of the excess energy while also ensuring that the puppy isn't going to be able to bite you again. This will allow the puppy to do some biting, but not at you, so you can both win in this situation.

Play in a Safe Manner

You should never be the one that plays roughly when your puppy bites. Your puppy is much more likely to bite at you and others when the playtime gets a bit rougher. You should also keep safe and never use your own hands as toys for the puppy. There are a lot of great toy options in many pet stores so go with those to stay safe. During the training process with your puppy, take the time to watch how your children pay with and around the puppy. Your children are not ready to take on the training responsibilities and you don't know how the puppy will react to your children.

Use The Spray Bottle

We mentioned this a bit above, but the spray bottle can be really effective to use when you are trying to train your puppy not to bite. You should wait until the situation is really severe, such as the puppy is biting all the time or starting to get deeper, and try some of the other options before. If the situation is this bad, you can carry around a spray bottle and use it any time the puppy bites.

For this to work properly, take the spray bottle, making sure it is going to spray out at the puppy rather than jet at them to avoid harming them. When they puppy bites you, say No! Firmly to them and then spray just a tiny bit o water at them. You should never use the spray bottle as a way to intimidate the puppy or make them feel scared of you when you are carrying the spray bottle. What you do want to do is reinforce that the biting is not acceptable and that you are not happy with this bad behavior.

In most cases, you will not need the spray bottle and even if you do, you will most likely just need it for a few days before the puppy sees that their behavior is wrong. As soon as you no longer need the spray bottle, go ahead and get rid of it and move on to other training methods to help your puppy adjust to behaving.

Reward the Good Behavior

Biting is a bad behavior that you don't want to reinforce, but if you spend all your time yelling at the puppy or getting mad at them, they are not going to understand what is allowed. Instead, they are going to get confused and may start acting out more because they think this is the only way to get your attention.

So, when it comes to the good behaviors of your puppy, make sure to praise it as much as possible. Whether they are being good at not biting or they are going through their tricks properly, take the time to let them know that they are doing a behavior that is seen as acceptable. Soon the puppy will start to strive to see your approval again and they will forget about doing the bad behavior, such as biting, and will instead focus on doing the good behaviors that you are teaching them.

It is important to start early in teaching your puppy that biting is not a good thing. This helps them to learn the rules right off the bat and ensures that you and others who come in contact with the puppy are not going to be harmed. Use the tips above to get that puppy trained off biting right away!

Chapter 9
How to Train a Puppy Not to Chew

Your dog is going to go through a phase where they want to chew up everything. This is their teething time and all this chewing makes their teeth and their gums feel a million times better. The issue comes up when they start chewing on all your favorite items in the house including your clothes, shoes, and other valuables.

In order to get your puppy to stop chewing through everything, you need to start understanding the reason behind their chewing. Dogs can chew for a variety of reasons, including teething, loneliness, boredom, and anxiety; all these reasons can show up after teething if you don't take the time to show your puppy that chewing on things is not accepted. Let's take a look at some of the reasons that your puppy is chewing so much and what you can do to help prevent this from happening.

The Teething Process

Your puppy is going to have a time in their life when they are teething. This can be difficult on them because they want to find relief, and often they will turn to some of your personal items to make this relief be felt. Don't just ignore the teething process unless you want a big mess on your hand. You instead need to make sure that the puppy has a variety of chew toys, including ones that are hard and ones that are soft. This allows them to still chew, but it is on something that you approve on rather than your really expensive new shoes.

When picking out toys, go for variety so the puppy is able to choose which ones feel the best for them. You should also be careful not to big out toys that have parts that can fall off or that the puppy can ingest, unless you are using food items as the chewing mechanism.

One option that a lot of people like is a big Kong toy that is made out of rubber and they can place peanut butter inside. This allows the puppy to work on their teething while trying to get to the yummy treat inside. Hard food items like ice cubes, dog biscuits, apples, and carrots. You can add these into the mix to keep the puppy interested and to prevent boredom from kicking in.

At times, the puppy may choose to ignore their toys and will chew up on some of your personal possession. It is best to keep these up high rather than assuming that the puppy is going to leave them alone like you asked. Always keep a few toys within easy reach so that the puppy can get to them whenever they feel the need to chew.

Preventing Other Issues with Chewing

Once the teething process is over, there is still going to be some want for the puppy to chew on things. Often they will do this in order to prevent boredom. Chewing is kind of like a game for them, just like fetching or going on a walk. It is your job to see this and provide other types of amusement for the puppy to keep them out of trouble. Luckily, there are a few things that you can do to keep this chewing at bay.

First, come up with a response for when the puppy does start to chew things up. It is never a good idea to start shouting or even hitting the puppy because this will just make the situation even worse. Usually a stern No! and reinforcing the good behaviors that you like from the puppy, while providing them with lots of good toys as replacements, can make a big difference in how much the puppy chews up your own items.

Next, make sure that you offer up a lot of different toys and switch them out on occasion. When a puppy is interested in their chew toys, they are less likely to want to go searching for something new and exciting to mess with. Try switching out the toys ever few months to keep them interested. Go for the toys that are sturdy and can take a bit of a beating; these will last a bit longer and you may be able to switch them out a few times.

Play with your puppy. Pent up energy can be a big reason why your puppy is trying to attack everything that comes near him. In order to get rid of this energy, you need to make sure that they are getting all this energy out in a more effective way. Take some time each day to play with the puppy, even if it's a simple game of fetch. Take them out on a long walk and let them run around and have fun. If you have a backyard, give them some time to run around back there until they are worn out. When the puppy is worn out, they are much less likely to start attacking your personal items and the chewing will often stop.

Give your puppy lots of attention. Sometimes the puppy may be acting out because they feel alone or bored. The best way to solve this is to give the puppy some one on one time. You can spend a bit of time each day going on a walk, playing with the puppy, or just letting them curl up next to you and get petted for a few minutes. The more time you spend with your new puppy, the more loved and appreciated they will feel. This translates into a happier time with your new puppy and fewer items being chewed on.

You are going to have to learn that all your valuables need to be kept off the floor when you're dealing with a brand new puppy. Everything is fair game to them until you teach the puppy that chewing is a bad thing. If you want to keep the item in good shape and working, you will need to learn how to pick up your messes off the floor.

Try confining the puppy when you're not home for a bit. Some puppies may be fine with leaving items alone when you're around, but the second you leave the house, they are tearing through the garbage, eating clothes, and attacking the furniture. This can be really frustrating as you are not home to make it all stop and can't really punish the puppy after the fact. One thing that you can try to do while gone, at least until the puppy understands that chewing is not allowed, is to use confinement.

You don't have to take it to the extreme of using a kennel, but find one room or corner of the room that belongs to the puppy while you are gone. Put up a little gate and leave a bit of food if you'll be gone for awhile, some water, and a few toys for the puppy to play with. this way, whatever the puppy does chew up will be left in this one area.

If you are running into trouble with getting your puppy to stop chewing and you have tried all the suggestions given, you may want to consider talking to a dog trainer. These professionals will work with you, often in your own home, to come up with a plan of training that will get your unique dog to stop misbehaving. Usually the issue is something simple and a few easy steps can help you to get this bad habit under control.

Chewing is a habit that most dog owners do not approve of. This is why it's so crucial to get started with the training against chewing at an early stage. Follow some of these steps, and it can become much easier to get your new puppy to behave rather than having them eat up all your personal items.

Chapter 10
Train a Puppy to Walk on a Leash

It is often beneficial to train your puppy how to walk with you on a leash. While some dog owners are able to walk with their dog without a leash, many areas could be dangerous for the dog without this control unit and you may live in an area that requires its use. No matter how often you plan to use the leash on your puppy, it is still a good idea to train them how to behave when wearing one. Here are the proper steps that you should take to train your puppy how to walk the proper way (without the pulling and tugging you see with other dogs) so you can both have a great walk.

Step #1:

Right when you bring the new puppy home you should start working with the leash. This helps the puppy to get used to the leash so it isn't some foreign object when they get older. To start, get a color that is pretty lightweight; you don't want the puppy to feel weighted down during this step.

Now, you will need to put this collar on the puppy for at least a few minutes several times a day. In the beginning, your puppy is not going to like having this object on them. It may feel weird to them and a bit heavy, and they are going to spend some time trying to take it off. Make sure they wear it on for at least long enough to settle down and quit scratching at it. If they don't seem to mind the collar, it is fine to leave it on for a bit. Over time, the puppy will get used to having the collar on and will stop trying to take it off.

Step #2:

After you have given your puppy some time to adjust to the new collar, it is time to introduce the leash. Make sure that the puppy no longer tries to take off the collar and can wear this pretty comfortably most of the time. This step is going to be similar to the last one in that you will just attach the leash to the color for a bit each day. Let the puppy drag the leash around with them, play with it, and get used to this new object.

When picking out the leash for this step, you don't have to get anything too fancy. Pick one that is light and that can take a bit of beating up since your puppy is going to explore with this new object. Over time, your puppy will get used to having the leash on and will run around the house without even noticing it is there.

Step #3:

You will need to give the puppy some time to get used to the new object following them around. You may find that this takes a few weeks. This is fine, just let your puppy play around and they can even use this as a toy. This gives them the ability to see what a leash feels like and to see that the leash is nothing to be scared of.

As the puppy becomes used to the leash, you need to start holding onto the leash. Up to this time, the leash has been an extension on the puppy, something to play with, but if you plan on holding the leash for walks and other outings, the puppy also needs to get used to you holding the leash. The first few times you hold the leash should be short practice rounds and find a way to make it fun. You can have the puppy just follow you for a few steps around the room so they get used to the idea of their human having the leash and that when the leash is on, you are the one in control.

Once you have given the puppy some time to get the feeling from this activity, it is time to make the walk a bit longer. Take the puppy outside and let them walk with you, maybe just going around the block. Use a lot of praise and even some treats when they are good. You will want to make the puppy walk either right beside you or right behind you a bit, but always have the leash be loose rather than taught. The puppy should never be pulling you along and you should never have to pull the puppy along. If the puppy behaves, reward them with a treat and lots of praise so they begin to understand what good habits they need while walking.

If the puppy insists on pulling on the leash, you must teach them this is not an acceptable behavior. You must also show them that they are not the leader and if they insist on being in front, you will not play along. Any time your puppy is performing in either of these two ways, stop the walk and refuse to go on until they agree to your terms. This helps to establish yourself as the alpha yet again and ensures that, with some more practice, the puppy is eventually going to do what you ask.

Over time, you will be able to take the puppy on longer walks. You can go on your daily jog or head out for some errands, knowing that your puppy will behave and do what you ask. This may seem like a lot of work in the beginning, but if you stick with it, you will find that your walks are much more enjoyable. You will be able to lead the dog, without a lot of pulling and tugging, in the right direction. Unlike other dog owners who are always fighting on a walk with their dogs, either pulling them forward or having the dog pull them, you and your puppy can have a nice walk with a loose leash between you two.

It is always best to teach your puppy this type of walking early on. This makes it easier to train them up right and once you get past the initial training, you will not have to worry about a rough walk again. Of course, if you do adopt an older dog, or failed to do the proper leash training when you first brought the puppy home, it is still possible to teach them how to do this kind of walking. It may take a bit to break them of their old habits and reteach the puppy what is acceptable, but all dogs can learn how to take a walk properly with the leash and you will find your walks are much more enjoyable than before.

Chapter 11
Agility Training

Another type of training that you can work on with your dog is agility training. This is a fun way to get your dog some exercise while helping them to become more obedient and do what you ask easier. Agility is basically a type of sport competition that is just for dogs; a mini Olympics that the dog can try out that includes jumping, going through tunnels, and other feats. When the dog is done with the work, they will be scored on how well they were able to do each task.

During agility, you are going to be the handler and will work right along with your dog to get through the obstacle course. Your puppy will have to learn how to listen to your commands in order to get through each phase of the obstacle course. When the puppy is well trained and knows how to listen to all of your commands, this can be a seamless endeavor that the dog enjoys, since they can let out a lot of energy, and you can show off your skill at training the puppy.

Agility training does take some time. You can't take out a brand new puppy and expect them to do well at these courses. You will be judged on how quickly your puppy can get through the course as well as how many mistakes they make along the way. A brand new puppy without any training will fail at all of this, but with some work and obedience training, your puppy will get better at this and be able to win the competition.

Best Dogs for Agility Training

While it is possible to use almost any kind of dog for agility training competitions, you will want to pick one that is easy to train and will do well with the speed. Right now, there are more than 150 breeds of dogs that are in agility sports, so it is pretty easy to get your personal dog into the mix; these breeds also include mixed breed dogs so don't think that this requires a purebred to compete. If you want to do these competitions or feel that your dog would be good at them, go ahead and start training them regardless of their bread.

In most cases, your puppy will not start performing for agility competitions until they are almost 2 years old. This is because younger puppies are more likely to get injured during the course, especially when it comes to jumping over hurdles. This gives you plenty of time to work on the obedience part of the competition as well as the speed before you have to start competing in the rest.

Starting Out The Training

While your puppy will not be allowed into the competitions until they reach a year old, it is possible to start training them before this date. The first thing you need to do is work on their obedience training. If the puppy has not mastered some basic commands and doesn't know how to follow what you ask them, it is going to be impossible to win in an agility competition. So, to start, work on the obedience commands like stay, heel, come, down, and sit.

Some who choose to go with agility competitions choose to take some training classes with their puppy. This allows their puppy to be around more dogs, something that will happen during the competition, and they can make sure that the commands are well known before the other training begins.

Once your puppy has had time to learn some of these basic commands, it is time to start working on the agility training. You may want to consider finding a group or class in your area to help out with this. While you will be able to do quite a bit of it on your own, it can be nice to meet up with other people who have done or who are doing these competitions and get some hints and tricks. This is a much better idea than trying to figure it all out on your own.

Start on The Obstacles

Before you can expect your dog to compete, you need to get them started out on the obstacles. They need to have at least a basic understanding of how to move around all these obstacles or go through them if you want to have any chance of them doing it during the competition. The more practice you can do with these with your puppy the easier time you will have during the competition. There are a few different types of obstacles your puppy will need to go through during the competition including the dog walk, the teeter totter, and the A-frame.

Let's start with the A-frame. This is a walkway that is going to be shaped like a teepee. The dog must learn how to go up an incline that is fairly steep and then go back down again using the other side. Next is the dog walk. For this one, the dog needs to be on a type of balance beam, usually a bit wider so the dog is able to use it, and there will be ramps on both sides for them to go up and down. And finally, the teeter totter looks like one from a children's playground and the dog must be able to walk across it, balancing their weight as they go. There are sometimes other obstacles, such as going through a tube and jumping over hurdles as well.

The three main obstacles are known as contact obstacles. These get their name because there are spots that the dog needs to touch on each side with one or more of their paws. The best way to get your dog to touch these areas is to practice by leaving a treat on the exact location they should touch. When the puppy touches the right place, they can have the treat. Do this each time you do a practice run so that the puppy makes it a habit to put their pay on the contact area and you can be awarded the points during competition.

At the beginning, keep all the obstacles low to the ground. Your puppy is not going to be able to leap over high obstacles without some practice and expecting the puppy to be able to do this is setting them up for injury. Go to the lower position, even if you have a bigger dog, and over time you can heighten the obstacle later on.

Now, bring out the leash to use as a lead for the puppy; later you will take this off and be able to get the puppy to follow your commands without it, but it is best to have the leash to start. State the command that you want the puppy to do, such as saying "A-frame" before leading the puppy over to that obstacle. For the first few trips, make sure to have some special treats around so that you can coax the puppy to try out this new obstacle.

Jumps

The obstacles are your first step. Once the puppy has had time to get used to these, you can give the jumps a try. Talk to your vet first to make sure that your puppy is old enough and well developed enough to do fine on the jumps without getting hurt. Just like with the obstacles, don't make the puppy jump too high. For a medium or large sized dog, you can keep the bar about an inch from the ground. Smaller dogs you may want to keep the bar right on the ground to prevent them from getting hurt. Over time, your dog will be able to jump higher and you can move the bar up a bit, but starting lower allows them time to get used to the idea and prevents them from becoming injured.

Just like with the obstacles, start the puppy using a leash on the jumps and to prevent the puppy from trying to go around your hurdle. You can give them a verbal command while doing the jump, like saying "big jump" to help them get used to this verbal cue before you take them off the leash. When you get to the jump, do a quick jump yourself and your dog is more likely to copy your movement and jump over the hurdle as well. The second the puppy follows your lead, offer up lots of praise and treats so they know they did a good thing.

Over time, your puppy is going to gain more confidence in themselves. Once they have mastered the lower height of the jump and can clear it without any issues, try raising it up a little higher. You can continue doing this until you reach the maximum height that is recommended for your puppy. Remember that you shouldn't try to rush through this too much and you should offer a lot of encouragement and praise to keep the puppy moving along.

Tunnels

This is a good obstacle to get started on because it is pretty simple for the puppy to learn. You should pick out a short tunnel so that the puppy is able to see to the other side. You can also bring along a partner who can stand on the other side of the tunnel and encourage the puppy to come through after you give your command and to hand out treats and praise once the puppy has made it through.

To get the puppy to go through the tunnel, lead them up to it and the command using the word "tunnel." At the same time, your helper should start offering treats and calling for the puppy to come through on the other hand. For hesitant puppies, you can throw in several treats to help them get going. Once your puppy has mastered the short tunnel, you can work in some different types of tunnels including ones that are longer and even tunnels that are curved.

Weave Poles

The weave poles can be a bit of a challenge because your puppy may not understand what they need to do. They will need to do a weave to get in and out of these poles and getting this down right is going to take some time and some practice. In order to get started with this obstacle, make sure to stagger out the poles, leaving them about shoulder width apart so the dog is able to get through.

Now, place a leash on your puppy and help lead them through the poles, offering a treat and some praise as you go. Once you are done doing this a few times and your puppy has started to get the idea, you can move these poles a bit closer together. This is going to start forcing the puppy to bend in their body a bit in order to get around the poles correctly. While this may take a bit of time to learn, eventually your puppy will be able to weave in and out of the poles without your assistance after just a simple command.

Pause Table

The pause table is a unique obstacle that is going to ask your puppy to either sit and stay or down and stay. They will need to get up on a table and perform either of these two commands quickly in order to finish out the race. Luckily, this table is usually about the height of your couch, so it doesn't include a lot of jumping to accomplish. You will be able to encourage the puppy to get up just by patting the surface of the table and then using a few treats to get them to come up to the right spot.

While getting the puppy up to the right spot is not too difficult, you may find that having the puppy stay put is a bit more of a challenge. Many dogs are going to be really anxious to go on to the next obstacle, but if you worked hard with your obedience training earlier on, they should have a good idea of how this command works and you can work to have that command still apply while on the table. Start out small if the puppy is too anxious and just have them stay for a second or two; you can build up to the bigger time limits later on until you get in at least five seconds at a time.

Getting it All Together

It is best to work on each of these obstacles on their own. This makes the agility training easier on both of you since you can just concentrate on one spot rather than worrying about how much is entailed in the whole thing. Once your puppy has mastered one part of the agility training, you will be able to move on to the next obstacle until the puppy has learned how to do all of these well.

The next challenge is to put all these tasks together. Your puppy is used to doing them separately, but they need to learn that all of these tasks have to be doe together, and they have to be done well and n a time limit.

The best way to get started is to simply link just two of the tasks together. You can combine the tunnel and the jump together and see how well the puppy does with this. First, give out the command so that your puppy will jump. Before they have the chance to get all the way to the ground when jumping, give the command to go through the tunnel while still moving on to the tunnel. Timing is going to be really important so that the puppy understands what they need to do next and will start moving on to the tunnel without hesitation.

Once you have gotten the puppy to do two parts of the obstacle course well, you can add on a third, and a fourth, and so on until it is all matched up well together. Make sure that you mix and match the course a bit, rather than doing the same steps over and over again. Each agility course is going to be a bit different so you want the puppy to become used to doing the obstacles in different orders. You will be given time to check out the obstacle course before the competition to get a feel for what to expect, but when you already train your puppy to follow your instructions rather than going in the same order for the obstacles, you already have a head start in winning.

Agility training can be another level that you take your training with the puppy. You can ensure that your puppy is going to listen to your commands no matter what. And agility training is a great way for the two of you to bond together and have some fun. Make sure to give your puppy plenty of time to learn the new tricks and don't push them too hard to make this happen. But if you take your time and listen to your puppy about how much they can handle, it becomes easier to get this done and you can have a great time as well!

Chapter 12
Keeping a Healthy Puppy

If you want the puppy to work on your commands and to be happy in your home, you need to make sure that they are kept healthy. There are many aspects that you need to put together to ensure that your puppy is being take care of properly. While we will spend a bit more time discussing each of these below, here are some basics of all the health care needs that you must give to your puppy to keep them healthy, happy, and ready to please you.

Feed the Puppy a Good Diet

The food you feed your puppy is really critical to their health. If you feed them an unhealthy type of dog food, or a lot of food off the table, you are depriving them of the good nutrition they need to keep active, listen to your commands, and to just stay healthy. Far too often dog owners are going to give their puppies the wrong kinds of food and wonder why the puppy is always sick, overweight, and just not listening.

There are some important things that you can keep in mind when it comes to feeding your puppy correctly. These include:

- Pick out food and treats that are high quality and well balanced. This will provide your puppy with all the nutrition they need.
- Limit the human food. Some types of human food can actually be harmful to your puppy since their metabolisms are different. Stay away from foods such as gum, chives, garlic, onion, alcohol, nuts, yeast dough, avocados, chocolates, raisins, and grapes.
- Keep their weight healthy—this will vary depending on the type of dog you have. A Saint Bernard can be much bigger than a Chihuahua so ask your vet for the right weight that is needed. If your dog is more than 20 percent of their ideal weight, they may suffer from a lot of health issues.
- Pick healthy treats. The treats that your puppy eats are just as important as their food. Pick ones that are low in calories but that have a lot of good nutrition packed into them.
- Lots of water. For the puppy to function properly and to keep energized, you need to provide them with lots of water. Make sure the water is cleaned out and fresh and clean out the bowel at least a few times a week. You can leave the water out all day to help the puppy get the amount that is needed.

A good diet is critical for keeping your puppy in good health for a long time. Follow some of these tips to ensure that you are providing the very best in nutrition for your puppy so they can live a long and happy life.

Do Some Grooming

Grooming is important to the health of your dog as well. It ensures that they are going to feel their best and that infections or disease are not likely to happen. There are a number of steps that you should take to groom your dog including:

- Do it regularly—take the time to brush the coat of your puppy to keep it healthy and encourage circulation in the puppy. This is the time to notice if there are any bumps or lumps on the puppy that weren't there before.
- Clip the nails—this is going to be hard because your puppy just won't like the nail clippers. The more you do the nail clipping, the quicker the puppy can get used to the idea. Take care to never trim up the quick part of the nail since this is full of nerves and will hurt the puppy.
- Brush the teeth—preferably you will do this each day to prevent plague from building up. Use a toothpaste that is meant for dogs because human toothpaste can be toxic. You can also use some chewing bones to help keep the teeth strong.
- Look at the ears—the ears should never have discharge or smell strange. The inner ear should look white, but if the dog is darker colored, the inner ear can sometimes be darker. If you are unsure, as your vet what to check for in your particular puppy.

Grooming your puppy is important to catching any health issues early and will help the puppy to feel good about themselves. These quick tips can help you to do this in just a few minutes each day.

Taking Good Care of the Puppy

The first thing you can do to take care of your puppy is to offer them a shelter. This can be any shelter that you choose, but make sure that the puppy is kept away from the elements as much as possible. Some families choose to let their puppy stay inside the house with them. This is a great idea because you won't have to worry about the cold or other elements harming your puppy. In the case of choosing to keep the puppy outside, you should make sure that they have plenty of water and food, shade for when it gets warm, lots of bedding for those cold nights, and a dog house that is well insulated so they stay warm.

For dogs that are outside, you shouldn't chain them up because they may get excited and pull too hard; causing potential neck and leg injuries in the process.

Next on the list is lots of exercise. Each breed is going to need a different amount of exercise in order to stay fit and get rid of their energy. Some of the bigger breeds, such a mastiffs, will only need a short walk around the block one or two times a day. Other dogs, like labs, may need to go on runs or spend a lot of time in the park. You should use this time to not only get the energy out of your puppy, but to bond with this new addition to your family. Remember, since you are getting rid of all the excess energy, you are also reducing the amount of naughty behavior the puppy will engage in.

After you have given your puppy all their vaccinations, it is time to socialize them. This helps them to learn how to behave around other animals as well as other people even when they aren't at home. You can also introduce them to a lot of different locations, such as the car, going to the park, or anywhere else that the puppy is allowed. Puppies like to be social so providing this extra step can help them to feel great and will get rid of some of that energy as well.

Providing Your Puppy with Good Health Care

You need to provide your puppy with the proper health care. This helps them to feel good and can ensure that you catch any issues that come up with your puppy before the issue gets any worse. The first part of health care that you should consider is finding a good vet. Your puppy needs to go for an exam at least once a year to get vaccinations and for the vet to find any health issues before they worsen. Find a vet you are able to stick with so that they can begin to know your dog and can catch up on health issues faster than someone who has never met your dog. When it comes to a puppy, make sure they go to the vet when they are 6 weeks old. During this visit, they are checked for overall health including ear problems, eye, lung, heart health, and hernias.

Next, you need to get your puppy all their vaccinations. This helps them to stay healthy and keeps them from getting other dogs and people sick as well. Most puppies should be given their rabies shots around 12 weeks old. In most areas, you will get a big fine if you don't vaccinate your dog properly, especially if they bite someone and get that person sick. If the puppy is going to spend a lot of their time outside, you really need to make sure that they get the rabies vaccine as well as their other vaccines at the right times.

You will need to consider whether you want to spay or neuter your dog. If you plan on breeding your puppy, this is not a procedure you are going to think about. But if you don't have any plans for breeding the puppy, getting them spayed or neutered can help get rid of some of their behavioral problems while also helping to decrease their risk of infections and tumors. You also won't have to ever worry about unwanted puppies coming later on.

Be on the lookout for any fleas that may infect your dog. When looking at their coat, check to see if the puppy has scabs on their skin, if they do a lot of scratching and licking, or if you see some dark specks in their fur. If any of these signs are present, go and visit the vet to get some medication to help cure this. Flea collars as well as some skin treatments can help to prevent fleas from attacking as well.

Each year when you go into the vet, you should have your puppy tested for heartworm. This is a disease that can be spread through mosquito bites so you really aren't able to prevent it too much. Many times you can give them a shot that lasts for six months or a tablet to help prevent heartworm from attacking.

Taking care of your puppy from the moment you bring them home and all through their years in your family is important to helping them to grow up big and strong. Make sure to follow some of the suggestions in this guidebook to help take care of your puppy and to give them a fantastic life.

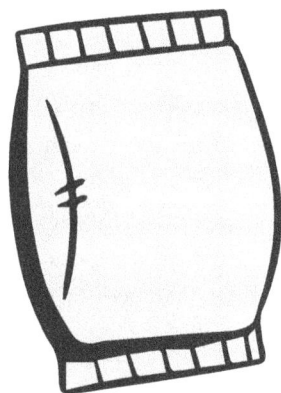

Chapter 13
Puppy Food Guide

The diet you provide for your puppy is going to be important to keeping them healthy and strong for a long time to come. Many dog owners assume that one brand of dog food will be as good as another. While the generic foods for humans simply offer a less expensive alternative, generic brands of dog food often are horrible for your dog to eat. This is one area where you will want to spend a bit more to ensure that your puppy is getting all the nutrition that they need out of their dog food and treats.

Understanding the Labels on Dog Food

To know whether your puppy is getting the right nutrition, you must read the label on the dog food. The first ingredient that MUST be on the label should be a specific meat. This meat can be chicken, beef, fish or whatever, but it needs to be the real thing. If you see chicken by-product or something else right beside the meat, this means the meat is not real and your puppy will not get the great benefits out of it. If another ingredient is placed first, such as bone meal, meat by-product, or corn, you should stay away from this kind of food because it is not good for the puppy.

So why should you pick out real meat rather than meat by-product. Aren't they basically the same thing? By-products are basically the leftovers of the meat, such as the feet, feathers, skin, hooves, and eyes. They are not good for dogs to eat and you should pick out another kind of food to keep your puppy healthy. In addition, if words like meat and animal are put in place of specific products like beef or chicken, run away and pick out another product.

Now that we know the importance of getting real meat in your dog food, let's take a look at how the labeling works. When looking at the label, the very first ingredient is the one that is found in highest concentration in the food. The other ingredients may be added in more for flavoring or to add in some more nutrition, but by weight, the first ingredient is going to take up the most room out of all the ingredients.

Make sure that you get dog food that doesn't have corn in it at all. Grains and corn are not good for your puppy and has been linked with bloating, joint swelling, and skin allergies in many dogs. If you don't have a choice, make sure that corn is listed as far down on the label as possible. Try to keep your dog on a grain free diet as much as possible. They are meant to enjoy meat all the time and grains and corn can make them very sick and don't provide the right kind of nutrition that your puppy needs.

How Much to Feed the Puppy

Once you have chosen the perfect dog food for your puppy, you are probably curious as to how much you need to feed the puppy. You want to make sure that they are well fed and not going hungry, but on the other hand, you don't want them to gain too much weight and have all those health issues. Here are some basics that you can keep in mind when it comes to how much to feed your puppy.

First 8 Weeks

During the first 8 weeks, the puppy should be kept with their mother. If the puppy is removed from their mother too early, they are going to have a lot of trouble adjusting to their new home and may cause some more issues. They are also more likely to have increased risk of illnesses. During this time, the puppy is going to get some good milk from their mother, milk that is full of nutrition and lots of antibodies to keep the puppies healthy.

Around three to four weeks, the puppy can be introduced to some solid foods, but will still have some of the mother's milk. You can mix together one part of the puppy milk with three parts o the food to help make it softer while the puppy gets used to the food. You will slowly keep doing this until the puppy is able to just eat the food without having it watered down.

6 to 8 Weeks

During this time, the puppy will need to be fed 3 to 4 times each day. The puppy is going to have nutritional needs that are different from the adult dog. Make sure that you are going with a puppy food rather than the adult version so that the puppy is getting the right amount of nutrition. Once the puppy reaches 8 weeks, you can probably move them down to just 2 feedings a day.

3 Months to 6 Months

This is the time when your puppy will begin to teeth. During this time, they may start to lose their appetite or become pickier about what they will like to eat. Keep offering up the nutritious food at both of the feedings. If the puppy is dealing with a stomach that is upset for more than two days, you should take them in to see the vet.

6 Months to 1 Year

Even though the puppy is going to look like they are all grown, you need to remember that they are still considered a puppy. Make sure to continue feeding them puppy food to give them the right kind of nutrition. You can discuss with your vet when is a good time to switch the puppy off the puppy food and over to an adult food so they continue to get the right nutrition at all stages. In this stage and all the others, you will only feed the puppy about two times a day unless directed otherwise by your vet.

As the puppy gets to their adult life, you will be able to change over the food to an adult type. This will provide the now grown up puppy with the right nutrition that they need to stay healthy and strong. If any health concerns come up, your vet may ask you to switch to a special kind of dog food. But if you are taking care of the puppy the way that you should, regular dog food will work out just fine.

Tips for Feeding Your Dog

Here are some basic tips that you can try out to help keep your dog healthy through the foods that you feed them.

- Feed the dog at the same time—this helps to keep the puppy on the same bathroom schedule each day. This also helps them to know when it is time to eat and they can know that the schedule stays the same. While most dogs will need to eat about twice a day, talk to your vet to see if your puppy has any special needs.
- Keep the food the same—your dog is not going to be able to handle their food changing each day; the digestive system is just not able to keep up with it and your puppy will start to feel diarrhea and upset stomach. Keep the brand and type of dog food as consistent as possible.
- Switch up slowly—if you do need to change up the dog food for some reason, such as switching to one for older dogs to deal with aging, you need to do it slowly. Start

by adding in just a bit to the regular food. Then slowly add in a bit more every few days until they are completely over to the new food.

- Keep the water nearby—as your puppy eats, they are going to get thirsty. Make sure that you keep some fresh water nearby for the puppy. Tray to replace the water once or more each day.

- Keep the bowels clean—this is important whether you are looking at the water or the food bowel. Keeping them clean helps to keep the dog healthy while they are eating.

- Never overfeed the puppy—only put out food during those two times of day that are considered feeding time and only give out the amount of food that your vet recommends. Leaving the food out all day long or giving out too much food and too many treats can make your puppy gain a lot of weight which is bad on their health.

- Make adjustments—if your puppy starts to gain weight, lower their food intake or add in some more activity to help them stay at a healthy weight.

- Try some sweet potatoes—this is great if your dog is dealing with loose stools. The sweet potatoes can act as a stool hardener and work naturally with the puppy. It is also better than some medicines that will constipate the puppy. You can also find sweet potato chips that are meant specifically for puppies at a pet supply store.

You can have a lot of control over the health of your puppy simply by the foods that you feed them. Make sure you pick out high quality food for the puppy, keep them active and moving around, and don't overfeed them and you will have a happy and healthy puppy that will love your family for a long time.

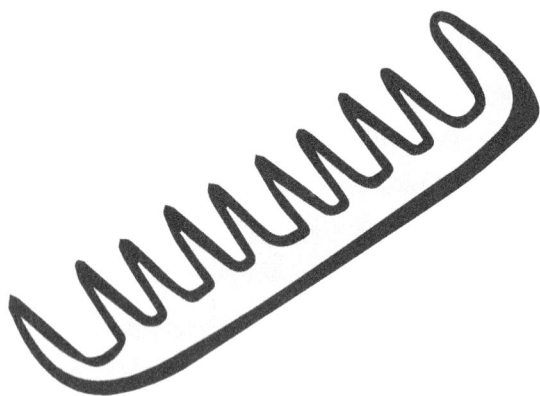

Chapter 14
Grooming

To help your puppy stay healthy and to promote healthy development, you need to make sure that you give the proper grooming to your puppy. You may be surprised at how well your puppy behaves and feels after a simple bath, hair brush, and having their nails cut. Many dog owners are worried about getting the grooming done properly and so will choose a professional to give them some help. As long as you are consistent with taking your puppy into a groomer, this is a great choice to help your puppy get the proper grooming that their health desires.

But choosing to do the grooming on your own can be a great choice as well. This process will allow you to get to know your puppy better than ever before and you can form a deeper bond once the puppy learns to trust you with their grooming needs. Understanding the proper grooming techniques is critical to helping your puppy, and if you've never groomed a puppy it might seem overwhelming. We are going to take a look at some of the basics of grooming so you can take good care of your puppy and do the grooming on your own.

Making Bath Time Fun

One thing that you must do often for your puppy is to give them a bath. This helps to clean their coat and ensures that dust and fleas don't get stuck inside and irritate them. But many times, the ordeal becomes a big chore for you because your puppy becomes scared of the bathtub. They will run away, cause a mess, and just be a big pain when it comes time to give them this all important bath. With the right steps though, you can turn bath time into a really fun time for the both of you. To make this happen, try out these steps:

1. Teach your puppy the command for the tub. You can go over to the tub and point at it while saying "tub." You may have to say this a few times to get the puppy used to the word, but as soon as they come over to the tub, you don't have to put them inside, give them a treat. Continue doing this until they are used to the new command.

2. Add in a rubber mat to get some traction. Add in some fun toys that the puppy will want to play with so that the tub looks like a fun place and not somewhere that is scary.

3. Put them in for a short amount of time. You don't need to have any water in at this time. You are just trying to get the puppy used to being in the tub and seeing that this is not such a scary place. Let them play for about five minutes before taking them out and going on with something else. Make sure to give the puppy a lot of attention while doing this so they know the tub is a good place. After a few times, your puppy will start to look forward to being in the tub.

4. Now start to run the water. At this time, you are just trying to get the puppy used to the sound of the water and how it feels. Don't let the tub fill up yet, but do allow the water to run.

5. Once the puppy is used to the water, you can start to fill the tub up a bit. Don't fill it all the way up so the puppy feels like they are drowning, but go to about ankle length to get them used to it. If the puppy is squirming, turn the water off, give them lots of praise and attention, and then offer up some treats to calm them down.

6. Give them a bath—once the puppy has gotten used to all the steps above, you will be able to give them the actual bath. By this point, you should be able fill up the tub and give your puppy a good bath without a lot of issues. Make sure to offer the puppy a lot of praise while you are giving the puppy a bath and give them a treat when they have done a good job.

Grooming the Puppy

Once the bath is done, you need to work on the rest of the grooming. This can be either a fun experience or one that turns into a nightmare depending on how you approach the whole thing with your puppy. Some puppies don't like grooming because their nails get clipped wrong and it hurts or because their owner is just unsure of how to make the experience more enjoyable. Keep in mind, the more enjoyable you can make the whole experience, including lots of praise and treats, the easier time you will have doing the grooming tasks with your puppy.

To start with in the grooming process is the brush. No matter what kind of puppy you have, you should start out with a brush, either puppy approved or human that is soft bristled. This will help with the sensitive skin of the puppy and will feel better. You should never use wire bristled brushes because this can cause some harm to the puppy. Over time, the softer puppy hair is going to shed and you will be able to use a better brush for your needs. Talk to a vet or a groomer to find out which brush is going to work the best for your needs.

During the grooming session, find a way to distract the puppy.

You can place some broth or some peanut butter into their bowl, or give them another treat, such as a bone, to enjoy while you are brushing their hair. You can then give the puppy a nice new coat without them having to sit still without distractions.

You will also need to work on the nails of the puppy. Keeping them short can help the puppy not cut into themselves when they scratch and will prevent them getting chipped or cracked. There are some special nail clippers that can help out with this process and which are strong enough to help you get the nail cut. You do need to be careful about using these clippers though. If you cut too far, you are going to cut into the nerves that are present right under the nail, and this is going to hurt the puppy; once they are hurt, you are going to have trouble getting them to do it again. If you have never clipped the nails of a puppy, talk to your vet or a groomer to learn the proper way to do this task.

Next on the list is to brush the puppy's teeth. Make sure to find a nice toothbrush that will be gentle on their teeth but still strong enough to get through all the gunk that gets in there. You should brush the teeth at least once a day, using a toothpaste that is approved for puppies; human toothpaste is not allowed for puppies because it can make them really sick.

When it comes to the teeth, find some toys that can help them out. There are some bones that the puppy can chew on that are nice for alleviating teething issues and which will help to clean out the teeth at the same time. Keep some of these on hand as a special treat for your puppy and to keep their teeth nice and clean.

Keep the ears of your puppy cleaned out as well. Lots of dirt and grime can get into the ear of your puppy so you need to clean them out while you are doing the rest of your grooming procedures. The ear should be mostly pink or white inside, although some dogs have darker ears because of their darker colors. Your vet will be able to show you what color is normal for your puppy and how to go about cleaning out the ear properly.

Grooming your puppy is important to keeping them happy and healthy. You need to get on a routine of helping your puppy get groomed as often as possible so they don't get sick or have to deal with ticks or fleas. Starting out on a grooming routine early on can help your puppy get used to these sessions and they will soon start to look forward to this quality time with you while feeling better with how great they look when done.

Chapter 15
What You Need to Know About the Vet

Your puppy will need to visit the vet on a regular basis to ensure that they are staying healthy. While it may seem like a good way to save money by not taking the puppy in, this could seriously risk the health of your puppy and the bills to help them out with a preventable disease or disorder is much worse than going in once a year. But it is important to be prepared for your visit to the vet to ensure your puppy is getting the best care possible.

Picking Out a Good Vet

Before your puppy gets very old, you should take some time to pick out a good vet. You want to find someone who has the best interests of your puppy in place. You want to find a vet who has a lot of experience, has gone to a good school, and who will be able to accurately figure out when your puppy is sick and how to make them feel better. Some of the most important things that you should do to pick out the perfect vet include:

- Check their credentials—before you agree to go with a vet, check out their credentials. Look to see where they have gone for their vet degree and ensure that their license is up to date. If there are other requirements for a vet in your area, ask to see these credentials as well to ensure that you have a vet who knows what they're doing.

- Get some reviews—you should ask around and see what some others have to say about this vet. Did they like the vet and enjoyed the good service. Was their a problem with how the vet got along with the puppy or something with the front desk not being friendly enough. Take the time to ask around, and even look online, to find out if this vet is the right one for you and your new puppy.

- See what animals they are used to working with—each vet is going to have different credentials for what they are able to provide care to. Some are fine with just small dogs while others may be able to handle all types of animals. Check with the vet to see what they are most comfortable with and then choose from there.

- See how they work with your puppy—after you have done some research, go and visit with the vet to figure out how they work with your puppy. You can take them in for a checkup or you can just go for a consultation to get to know them. See if your puppy seems comfortable around the vet and how well you like their work.

- Check for procedures they are able to do—some vets are able to provide surgeries and other special services to your puppy while others may not have the right credentials in order to do this. You should check to see what the vet is able to do and determine if you are comfortable with that or if you would like to find a vet that can do it all in one place.

- Make sure you are comfortable with their work—if you don't feel comfortable with anything the vet is doing during your visit, look around for a new vet. It doesn't matter how many credentials the vet has, you don't want to make yourself or the puppy uncomfortable by keeping the relationship going. Pick someone you feel incredibly comfortable with so that you can continue that relationship for a long time to come.

Picking out the right vet for you and your new puppy can be a big decision. Take your time and look at a lot of reviews to figure out who will work well for you and your puppy to give them the best health possible.

Your Puppy's First Exam

The first visit that you take with your puppy to the veterinarian is going to be full of a lot of information. You are going to take the time to check out your puppy as well as educate yourself about the proper way to take care of the puppy so they grow up big and strong. There are two things that you should bring with you to this first exam. The first thing is any health records that are available for the new puppy. If you have a puppy that is brand new from a breeder, bring in some information from those first few visits as well as any information you were able to get on the parents. If you got the puppy from a shelter, bring in all these records as well. This can help the vet get a clear view of how the puppy is doing and if there are any potential issues they should watch out for. The second thing that you should bring is any concerns or questions that you may have for the vet.

During your first visit, the vet is going to spend a lot of time looking over the puppy. They want to check out as much as possible to ensure that the puppy is in good shape. They will start out with the temperature and weight of your puppy as well as the breathing and pulse rate. This helps the vet to see if the puppy is at the ideal weight and health for their age or if there is a need for concern.

Next, the vet will move on to the ears. This is an easy place for the puppy to get a lot of dirt and grime inside and they won't be very happy if they get an ear infection. They will check the look and the smell and may prescribe some medication to keep them safe. The gums and mouth are important as are the skin, nose, and eyes of the dog. The vet is going to be very thorough to make sure that all parts of the body are healthy for your puppy.

During this visit, the vet is going to work to help your puppy have fun. The relationship between your vet and your puppy is just as important as the one that you hold with your puppy because you will need to go and visit them quite a bit. If the puppy is not comfortable with the vet, you are going to have some issues during these visits and the vet may not be able to give the right amount of attention that your puppy needs.

You also need to be a big part in this positive interaction. You should never encourage your puppy to be shy or aggressive when they are near the vet, or anyone else for that matter. You need to keep upbeat and use a lot of praise during the visit. When your puppy feels that you feel comfortable with the vet and that you see this as a good place to me, they are going to be more willing to go through the exam.

Even after the first visit, there are going to be a lot of other times that you go to the vets. First, you will need to go at least once a year for a checkup. This allows the vet to visit with you about your puppy, check if any of their health conditions have changed, If the vet is concerned about anything at these visits, they will recommend that you come back again in so many months to recheck the situation. Write down the appointment and don't forget about it because this could make a bit difference in the health of your puppy.

Outside of these visits, you may have a few emergency situations when you will need to take the puppy in. Some of these situations may include:

- Your puppy has an allergic reaction. If this happens, make sure to check them for hives or swelling around their face or on the belly.
- An injury to the eye, even if it doesn't seem like much
- Respiratory issues—this would include issues such as near drowning when swimming or taking a bath, trouble with breathing, and a chronic cough.
- Signs of pain—this would include issues such as loss of their appetite, restlessness, lethargy, higher body temperatures, labored breathing, and panting.
- Any signs of being poisoned including those from human medication, snail and rodent bait, or ingesting antifreeze.
- Lacerations or wounds that are bleeding and open as well as any bite from an animal.
- Collapse, fainting, or seizures.
- Thermal stress meaning that the dog has been either too hot or too cold, even if you think the puppy has recovered.
- Any type of trauma, like a hit from a car.
- Diarrhea or vomiting that occurs more than three times in an hour.

If any of these signs show up, you must take the puppy into the vet right away, regardless of when their last appointment occurred. These can be indicative of a big issue to your puppy and you need to get them taken care of before it gets any worse. Also, any time that you have some concerns with your puppy, even if the concern is not listed above, take them in for a checkup to be safe.

The vet is your best friend when it comes to keep your puppy safe and sound for a long time to come. Make sure that you get in for all the right checkups and that you find the perfect vet to help you keep your puppy safe and healthy for many years to come.

Visiting the Vet for a Lifetime of Health

While the first visit is really important, you still need to make sure to go and visit the vet routinely throughout their life. It is not enough to go through for a few months and then just wait until your puppy gets sick and really needs the vet. You need to go on routine visits to the vet to ensure that your puppy is given the best care and that they get treated long before a little health issue becomes a big one.

It is recommended that you take the puppy to the vet at least once a year after their first year. This gives the vet some time to look them over and ensure that they are still developing how they should. You can use this time in order to ask any questions that come up and to learn new techniques to keep your puppy healthy. Your vet can check for age related health concerns and may suggest a different level of dog food or other nutrients to help them to continue their great development.

Visiting the vet is critical to keeping your puppy healthy and happy. When you visit the vet, you will be able to catch any early problems or prevent them for the overall health of your puppy. Follow these simple guidelines to understanding what you should do and expect at a vet visit so it's not so intimidating and can be a great experience for all involved.

Chapter 16

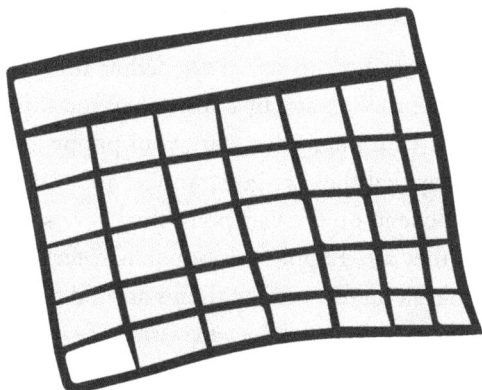

Schedules and Routines for Puppies

Before we end this guidebook, we are going to spend some time talking about how important a great routine and schedule can be for your puppy. It is never a good idea to just let the puppy come into your home and do whatever they want. They will get used to this and not be able to understand commands or what obedience training that you would like. A routine helps the puppy to feel safe, learn commands easier, and to behave better than ever before.

Coming up with a routine for your puppy may seem like a task that is difficult to overcome. But if you just put the puppy on your personal schedule and stick with this as much as possible, you will find that it is much easier to work this in with the puppy. And this schedule is so important to helping your puppy know where their place in life is and allowing them to do better with training. So let's get started with creating an amazing schedule for your puppy.

Why is a Schedule so Important

Before we go into how to set up a schedule for your puppy, let's take some time to look at why consistency and routine is so important for your puppy. To start, your puppy is a creature of habit. The way that they are going to feel about their world will completely depend on the viewpoint they have shaped based on how happy they are. Puppies are not able to feel happy or have a positive outlook on life and the things around them, if they don't have a stable routine with a lot of consistency.

Many times, you may have to deal with a puppy that is aggressive, shy, or difficult to train. You may bring in the professionals and wonder why you just aren't seeing the results that you would like. Often the issue is that the puppy doesn't have a routine and they are developing a negative outlook on life because they don't get those habits that they like. Any puppy that doesn't get the right consistency and routine through their lives will feel depressed, anxious, and stressed and often these emotions lead them to act out.

If you are dealing with a puppy that won't behave, take a look at their schedule. Is their schedule full of routine and pretty easy to predict. Do they learn quickly and have their meals, bathroom breaks, walks, and other things at about the same time each day with a lot of consistency. For those dogs that aren't behaving, the answer is probably no to all of these.

The best way to make sure that your brand new puppy, or an older dog that is exhibiting bad behaviors, to behave how you would like is to implement a new routine. While it is best to do this when the puppy is young, it is never too later to get started on a great routine. Just start introducing new things into your puppy's life, one at a time, until the whole routine is in place. Over time, you will see that the puppy really loves having this routine and this simple step, even though it takes some time, can make a big difference in your relationship with the new puppy.

So no matter what stage you are at with your puppy, make sure to get that routine in.

This routine is a great way to help your puppy to feel wanted and allows them to enjoy their natural instinct for having habits. Try to stay on this schedule as much as possible to avoid confusion, as well as bad behavior, with your new puppy.

Getting into a Daily Routine

For the routine to work, you need to implement it into your daily life. If you don't use the routine each day, you will find that the puppy is not used to what is going on and it will be harder to get them trained or used to the way that your life runs. There are many things that you can include into your puppy's daily life to help them learn what the routine will be and how they should behave each day.

Each part of your new puppy's life should be on a routine. You should make sure that they have feeding times that are the same each day, that they go on a walk at about the same time, that bed time stays consistent, and that they get some playtime or training each day. When the puppy begins to know what they should do each day and what they can expect, it is much easier to get them to behave and act the way that you would like.

To get the daily routine going, you need to decide what tasks will be done with the puppy each day and when you would like to do them. If it helps you to stay organized, consider getting out a planner or a calendar and writing down each of the tasks that you would like to complete each day and the approximate times they should be done. This can help you to get started for the first few days and you can move things around to get the timing and the activities that work best in your schedule. After a few days, you will have this down and it won't be necessary to keep a chart, but this is a good way to ensure you aren't forgetting about something important and that you keep things in order.

Starting Their Feeding Routine

You should have a routine for when the puppy is allowed to eat. This allows the puppy to know that they are going to be fed, and allows you to still be the alpha in the family because you won't allow the puppy to eat before you. This routine is not important just for the mental and emotional wellbeing of your puppy, but also so that the metabolism of the puppy is able to get onto a pattern and learn when the puppy will be allowed to eat.

When it comes to feeding, try to keep everything as consistent as possible. Put the food in the same area each day, ensure that the puppy is comfortable, have the food set out at the same times each day, and feed them the same kind of food all the time. You should never just leave the food sitting out for the puppy to choose when meal time is. This will undermine your chances of being the alpha and with food always readily available, you will have an issue with weight gain in your puppy.

Walking and Bathroom Routine

You will need to set up a routine for your puppy to go outside and even to the bathroom. When you get into a routine with the exercise, your puppy will know that if they just behave until you get home, they will get to go outside and play and run out the energy. Without the routine, the puppy will assume that they never get to go outside, because maybe you go out or maybe you don't for a few days, and they will start to get into everything and cause a mess. Puppies like to wear out their energy and need to be outside for walks and other activities. Make it a part of your routine, even if you just go out for 30 minutes on a walk after work, and you will be amazed at how quickly your puppy will stop misbehaving and get into the routine.

You also need to get into a routine with the puppy going to the bathroom. Now you won't be able to predict each time the puppy needs to go, but you can take some steps to ensure that they are getting let out as much as possible in a routine. For example, when you first get up in the morning, take the puppy out. When they are done eating, let them go out. When you get home from work or right before you go to bed, allow the puppy to go outside and relieve themselves. This can make it a whole lot easier to train your puppy and prevent them from having accidents inside the house.

Routines with Training

Often, the routine that your puppy is going to form is founded by the way that you and others in the home are handling the puppy. This means that you need to keep your training, as well as the commands that you are using, as consistent as possible. If you make the rule that the puppy is not allowed on the furniture, that is a rule that you and everyone else needs to follow at all times. If you have taught the puppy various commands, make sure these commands lead to the same results each time so that the puppy knows what to expect.

You may need to take some time to discuss this with your family before training the puppy. Everyone needs to train and act in the same way regarding the puppy. This is the only way that the puppy can get on a good routine and start to feel like they belong.

Making Changes When Needed

While it is important that you keep your routine as simple and consistent as possible, there are times when the routine may change up a bit. You may need to change your hours at work, or you may go on a trip somewhere and the dog will come along. There are many reasons that the schedule may need to change, but when it does, give your puppy the time and patience to get all this figured out. Your puppy is going to be used to having one schedule and won't want to change it up because this is just not as comfortable. So you have to take it slowly and help your puppy get used to the idea that something does need to change a bit.

If you do need to change up the schedule or introduce a new item or change into the environment of your puppy, you need to do it at a gradual pace. Also, only introduce one thing that is new at a time rather than trying to change a whole bunch at once. This is just going to upset the puppy and can make training them, or getting them to behave, much more difficult.

Once you introduce one thing that is new, take the time to see how your puppy likes the new item. If they are a little slow at taking it on, give them some more time. Once they have gotten used to this new routine, you can add in something else or just have this be your new routine for good.

A routine is really important for your puppy. It helps them to feel secure in what they are doing and keeps them from getting confused about what is going on in life. It is critical for you to get the routine set up quickly to help make training as well as life with your puppy as easy as possible.

Conclusion

Bringing a new puppy into your home is a big step for any family no matter who you are. You may have a lot of excitement for this new addition and can't wait to introduce them to your home. Going through the proper training techniques can help you to gain control and get your puppy to act in a way that is conducive to your way of living. Training should be done as soon as you bring the puppy home so that the rules can be established early on and your relationship with the puppy is understood from the beginning.

If you have never trained a puppy, the idea of getting them to obey you and do the work that you want in your home can seem scary. But simply following the easy tips in this guidebook, you will see that training your puppy does not have to be a hard endeavor. You just need to be the one in control and help guide your puppy, while keeping it fun, to the behaviors that you see as acceptable.

When you are ready to train your puppy and to see the results necessary to have a happy new life with the puppy, take a look through this guidebook. It provides all the tips you need to keep your puppy in line and acting the way that works best with your family dynamics.

Want more puppy training tips?

Get monthly dog training tips, 15% off your first order on our premium puppy pads, our exclusive House Training Confidence Guide, more discounts, exclusive offers, updates, and much more!

JOIN BULLDOGOLOGY CLUB (FREE)
https://www.bulldogology.net/join

www.ingramcontent.com/pod-product-compliance
Lightning Source LLC
Chambersburg PA
CBHW051901090426
42811CB00003B/413